£7.50
4942

THE MANOR HOUSES OF BURTON AGNES
AND THEIR OWNERS

by

Margaret Imrie

D1342475

HUTTON PRESS

1993

Withdrawn

Accession Number T031827

Class Number 4942

Published by the Hutton Press Ltd.
130 Canada Drive, Cherry Burton, Beverley
East Yorkshire HU17 7SB

Copyright © 1993

No part of this book may be reproduced, stored in a
retrieval system or transmitted in any form, or by
any means electronic, mechanical, photocopying,
recording or otherwise without the prior permission
of the Publisher and the copyright holders.

Printed and bound by
Clifford Ward & Co. (Bridlington) Ltd.
55 West Street, Bridlington, East Yorkshire
YO15 3DZ

ISBN 1 872167 49 7

CONTENTS

ACKNOWLEDGEMENTS

I am very grateful to the Hon. Mrs. Susan Cunliffe-Lister who willingly agreed to the idea of this book, helped with the text of the final chapter, searched the family albums for suitable photographs and gave permission for new ones of Burton Agnes Hall and contents. I have also had much help from everyone else at the Hall, particularly Mr. Keith Hawkins, who has a fund of information gathered from 50 years work in the house and estate, Sr. Vicente Arroyo, Mr. Pablo Garcia, and the guides, Mrs. Josie Harrison, Mrs. Jean Leach, Mr. Walter Leach, Mr. Robert Slater, Mr. Cyril Stephenson, Mrs. Wendy Sykes, Mrs. Joyce Theakstone and Mrs. Barbara Wilson who have variously told me stories of the house, the family and the village and made available the results of their own researches. Mr. and Mrs. Adrian Jones kindly allowed access to the roof of their home, the Gatehouse, so that other photographs could be taken.

For information on the office of Sheriff I wish to thank Mr. Richard Marriott. Miss Pamela Martin, Mrs. Jenny Stanley and the staff of the Beverley Local Studies Library have been unfailingly helpful as were those of Staffordshire Archive service. Thanks also to Mr. Brian Dyson, the Archivist, the Brynmor Jones Library, University of Hull, for his help and permission to photograph documents and to Mr. Roland Wheeler-Osman of the University of Hull Photographic and Copy Service.

Dr. Barbara English gave advice in the early stages and Drs. David and Susan Neave read the manuscript, pointed out errors of interpretation, have been particularly helpful on the technicalities of presentation, and have always been ready to answer queries. I am very conscious that there is much yet to discover about the Burton Agnes houses and their owners and the omissions mistakes that remain are mine.

Finally my thanks to my family who have endured my preoccupation for some time and particularly to my husband Mike who has also helped with the illustrations and my son John who taught me how to use a word-processor and answered many maternal cries of help with patient forbearance.

Margaret Imrie,
Leven.
May 1993

INTRODUCTION

This is the story of the two manor houses of Burton Agnes, now a small village of about 350 inhabitants straddling the A166 between Driffield and Bridlington in the old East Riding of Yorkshire, and, in part, of the family that has owned them and their estates since the 12th century.

Burton Agnes Hall, built in the early 17th century, is justifiably considered to be one of the most attractive historic houses open to the public in England, and one of the least well known. Situated off the main tourist routes it gets very little national publicity; consequently its visitors are amazed by the quality of the building and its contents and delight in the special atmosphere of a lived-in family home. Whilst these can be savoured in half a day (though there is so much to see that people come back again and again) the history of the house and its Norman predecessor, still standing close by, is a different matter.

I started to write this book because, as a guide at the house, I felt that if I tried to tell more than a small part of its story during the usual tour, I was in danger of inducing a severe attack of information fatigue, but I knew that many people wanted to be able to find out more at their leisure.

In order to understand the houses one needs to know enough about their occupants to appreciate their requirements when they built and, over the years, altered them and also something of the times in which they lived; but this book does not attempt to be a definitive history of the owners. That would now be very difficult to write as most of their personal papers were destroyed or sold in late 1940s. Fortunately they were available to the Rev. Carus Vale Collier who, early in the present century, compiled a family history which gives facts and dates though not much insight into their lives. However there are enough clues in what remains, particularly in the legal documents kept by the family solicitors and now deposited in Hull University Archives, and the various public records, to flesh the story out a little, though of course there is a lot more to be discovered.

Over the years the family fortunes have waxed and waned. They bought land when they were rich and sold it when they were poor. They built great houses which they altered and modernised and then allowed to fall into disrepair. They looked after their tenants and treated them badly. They co-perated with their neighbours and quarrelled with them. They were magistrates, sheriffs, deputy lieutenants and occasionally members of parliament; their lives were inter-woven with the history of England. They fought against France in the 14th century and Germany in the 20th. In the 15th century they fought the Yorkists and in the 17th they fought each other. Though they nearly lost the property at this time for political reasons, and it was touch and go at the beginning of the 19th century, this time because of financial recklessness, they have always clung on to the house through thick and thin and six changes of name as, from time to time, the male line ran out.

The estate was owned by the Griffiths and their successors the Boyntons for nearly 600 years so their names predominate. Sir Henry Griffith was the builder of the Jacobean house but his son was the last of his line and it passed via his sister to the Boyntons, When the son of the last of the Boyntons, Marcus Wickham-Boynton, inherited it in 1947, neglect and wartime privations had left it in a sorry state.

The result of his years of loving restoration is a house structurally sound, oak panelling richly glowing and rooms filled with the fine furniture he gradually acquired to replace the 'moderate stuff' that was there. He was also a collector of French paintings, bronzes, Chinese porcelain and other works of art which fill the house to the amazement of the unprepared visitor who finds himself looking at canvasses by Renoir, Pissarro, Matisse, and many other famous artists of the Impressionist and Post-impressionist periods.

In 1977 Marcus Wickham-Boynton, to ensure its future, gave Burton Agnes Hall and its contents to a specially formed preservation trust. On his death in 1985 his heirs, his distant cousins the Cunliffe-Lister family, inherited the estate and the use of the house as a family home. They are carrying on where he left off and in 2002, when he is 25, it will all become the responsibility of Simon, who can trace his ancestry back through 26 generations to Roger de Stuteville who built the Norman manor house in about 1174. In the meantime his mother, the Hon. Mrs. Susan Cunliffe-Lister, is in charge. A multi-talented lady she has already transformed the walled-garden and under her care it and the house are thriving.

The crossroads at Burton Agnes showing Elizabeth Boynton's almshouses built 1709 and demolished when the road was widened, 1939.

The crossroads today with village pond.

7

LIBRARY
BISHOP BURTON COLLEGE
BEVERLEY HU17 8QG

CHAPTER ONE
THE ORIGINS OF BURTON AGNES

The Domesday Book

"In Bortona with three outliers, Gransmoor, Harpham, Boythorpe 25 carucates of land taxable, which 15 ploughs can plough. Morcar held this as one manor before 1066 and it was then worth £24; now one person pays rent of 10s. to the king. The whole manor one league long and as wide. To this manor belongs the jurisdiction of these lands – Langtoft 3 carucates, Haisthorpe 4 carucates, Thwing 8 carucates, (Potter) Brompton 3 carucates, Thornholme 7 carucates. In all there are 25 carucates taxable which 14 ploughs can plough. Now waste".

In 1086, King William I, after 'much thought and very deep discussion with his council', ordered a detailed inventory to be made of the land he had conquered twenty years previously for the purpose of maximising his rents. The Norman system of government he had imposed assumed that the land and everything on it belonged to the king. Commissioners were sent all over the country and their findings were recorded in the Domesday Book, the above being the entry for Burton Agnes.

For a short paragraph it tells us a great deal. First of all the village was in existence in 1086 and had been for some time, the name 'Burton' is Anglo-Saxon meaning a fortified farmstead and the Saxons came in the fifth century, after the Romans had left. In fact Roman remains have been found nearby and there are prehistoric graves on the Yorkshire Wolds above the village so it is clear that the position of Burton Agnes attracted people to it from earliest times. This is not at all surprising; what they needed was an inexhaustible supply of drinking water and a defensible site and Burton Agnes with its steep chalk hillside rising directly from springs (which now feed the pond) was ideal.

In the Domesday Book Burton Agnes was a manor and belonging to the manor were the small settlements of Gransmoor, Harpham and Boythorpe. In general terms a manor comprised a village and its land tenanted by a lord of the manor in the property-holding line of succession from the king and had a manor house lived in periodically by the lord and his household, and the much smaller houses of the villagers. It may or may not have had a church and a mill. The other places named in the entry, Langtoft, Thwing, Potter Brompton and Thornholme had decided in pre-conquest times that all disputes and incidents of law-breaking in their villages should be brought before the manor-court at Burton Agnes thus giving it jurisdiction over a large area and making it an important local centre.

Morcar had been lord of the manor but now 'one person pays 10s. to the king'. Where was Morcar? He had been the Saxon Earl of Northumberland but after a short period of co-operation with William he and other northern landowners rebelled, were conquered again, and met various unfortunate fates. Morcar was shipped off to Normandy and imprisoned before being returned to Winchester where he died. The king now became lord of the manor and until he decided on a tenant it was administered by his sheriff who paid a lump sum known as 'farm of the shire' to the king and then made his own profit from local taxes.

There cannot have been much to be made from Burton Agnes. The manor, which in 1066 was worth £24, was worth 10s. in 1086, being described as 'waste', as were Driffield, Kilham, Rudston, Barmston, Beeford and many others round about. Clearly something dreadful had happened. Wiliam, had put down Morcar's rebellion with a great ferocity known to history as 'the harrying of the North', his soldiers rampaging over the countryside burning the villages and killing the villagers. In 1085, just when the land had recovered somewhat and immediately before the visit of the Domesday commissioners it was again laid waste because of a threatened invasion from Denmark, William not wishing the Danish army, should it arrive, to be able to live off the land. However by 1086, as one man is paying rent to the king, there must be some agricultural activity however small. It is thought that the rent-payer may have been Geoffrey Baynard who was Sheriff of York during the reign of William II.

The new tenant-in-chief was Robert de Brus, obviously a Norman from his name, though it later looked more English (or Scottish) when it was spelt Bruce. He was one of the many new French speaking landlords of England, for after the short period of uneasy coexistence native owners' rebellions had been nationwide. England was parcelled out amongst William's trusted supporters, the men who had commanded his invasion force.

It is unlikely that Robert de Brus lived at Burton Agnes, he may only have visited it rarely, if at all; he paid his rent by providing fighting men, knights, for his king and these men he settled on his land as minor lords of the manor from which they got a living in return for so many days of fighting availability. This was the feudal system so named because one knight lived off a 'knight's fee'; his villagers, always having to be ready to follow their lord into battle, formed the base of the social pyramid.

The Thwing and Lumley families later became the tenants-in-chief by inheritance through Robert's grand-daughter, but these do not concern us further as they were remote from the day to day life of the manor.

Who was Agnes?

Villages grew up round many of the Saxon burtons and they needed distinguishing names; Burton Fleming, Cherry Burton, Bishop Burton, Brandesburton are all quite close to Burton Agnes, but it is one of only a handful of places in England incorporating a personal name not the patron saint of its church. So who was the lady who gave her name to the village? Sadly no-one now can be certain as Agnes was a popular name in those days, but a likely candidate is the daughter born in 1120 to Stephen of Aumale, Lord of Holderness, and one of the most powerful men in the country. She married Adam de Brus, son of Robert, and it is probable that the manor was part of her

9

dowry after the death of Adam and would then be known as Agnes's Burton. The name first appeared on a deed witnessed in about 1175 and early in the next century it was written variously as Anners or Anneys Burton. It was Burton Agnetis in 1255, Agnes Burton in 1697 and then settled into Burton Agnes which is no doubt what it will now remain.

CHAPTER TWO
THE NORMAN MANOR HOUSE

The Stutevilles

In Saxon times the manor house stood out from the rest of the buildings in the village because it was larger but apart from that consisted, as they did, of one room with a hearth in the middle, the smoke finding its way out through the thatch. The end furthest from the door was the lord's where he and his family ate and retired for the night, and his household had the rest of the available space.

About a hundred years after the Conquest the manor house was redesigned. Since everybody held their land by reason of being able to fight for their immediate overlord, and since fighting was the usual way of settling disputes, the house was constructed with an eye to defence and the withstanding of a siege. Now known as 'first-floor hall type' one such was built at Burton Agnes in about 1174 by Roger de Stuteville, the younger son of a family which owned much of the North Riding of Yorkshire. His father had fought for the king at the Battle of the Standard against the Scots and his brother was Sheriff of York. It is not known how Roger came by Burton Agnes but presumably it was through one of the land exchanges which were common at the time.

The new house must have replaced an earlier Saxon one no trace of which remains above ground. Though now heavily disguised on the south and east sides by a brick facing and sash windows the core of Roger's house still stands today close by the great house that in turn eventually replaced it as the lord's residence. An excellent example of this type, of which about twenty now remain, it was built at a time when not only local skirmishes between powerful lords were frequent but also when the sons of Henry II were rebelling against their father and revolts supporting one or other side were breaking out all over the country. It was as well to make one's house as safe as possible.

The three-foot thick walls were constructed of limestone with chalk rubble infilling, the limestone perhaps brought from the quarry at Newbald which provided the building blocks for many local Norman churches, possibly including the village church close by which had been started 20 years previously. The chalk was quarried on the estate. For greater security the 'hall', still the main living and sleeping area for all the occupants, was raised above a ground-level 'undercroft' with its doorway reached by an external staircase. This gave the advantage to the defender standing at the top although it is possible that the steps were detachable wooden ones which could be brought into the hall when danger threatened.

In the corner by the door is the spiral staircase which gave access to the undercroft from the hall. This was lit by round-headed windows too narrow for anyone to climb through but widely splayed on the inside to let in as much light

The Norman manor house: the undercroft.

as possible. One of these on the north wall has been restored. The most remarkable feature of the undercroft is the vaulted ceiling resting on three piers decorated with waterleaf capitals. The ribs of the vault are made of white chalk (as is the architrave of the hall door) and it has much in common with the crypt of St. Mary's Church, Beverley.

None of the original hall windows remain but assuming that they were the same as other contemporary manor houses they were at least double the size of those in the ground-floor room with a stone bar down the centre where the shutters could be fastened. There is evidence that the window which lit the lord's end was larger than the rest which was the usual pattern. It is very unlikely that the windows contained glass; during the day the weather was kept out by a lattice made of wicker or thin shavings of oak and at night shutters were bolted across the openings. Places by the huge fireplace in the north wall must have been eagerly sought after when the winter storms blew. The roof would almost certainly be thatched with straw or reeds.

Where was the cooking done? Originally on the hall fireplace, but later like other houses of the period, there would be a detached kitchen close by the main house. This was to limit the damage when the kitchen caught fire, a fairly frequent occurrence.

Though there was plenty of fresh water only a hundred yards distant in the springs at the bottom of the hill this was too far for safety and so a deep well was sunk close to the house to tap the underground stream before it emerged. To complete the defences there must have been a wall round the house and the well but nothing of it now remains.

While building his house, Roger also added a north aisle to the church, converting the original wall of the narrow nave into an arcade of three arches. At that time, and indeed until very recently, everyone believed in an eternity in the fires of hell as a real and nasty possibility for one's afterlife and anything done for the church might be thought of as an insurance policy.

Life in the Norman Manor House

Like all people of his standing Roger had other manors elsewhere and spent his year (when not fighting) travelling round them. This dispersal of property had been a cunning ploy of William the Conqueror's to prevent anyone building up too powerful a land base in one area. While at Burton Agnes the house would be filled with the furniture and utensils that he brought with him and he would dispense hospitality to all his neighbours. Dinner, eaten towards the end of the morning, was the principal event of the day; Roger, his family and guests of rank, sat at the High Table, which was placed at the end of the hall furthest from the door, facing his household who ate at trestle tables put up lengthwise along the hall. At night, the tables and stools having been stacked against the wall, the senior members of the household bedded down on the hall floor, the lower ranks going down to the undercroft. Until the 16th century the only females in these establishments were the wife and daughters of the lord and the one or two ladies attending them.

We now have to guess how the de Stutevilles disposed themselves. Either they slept at their end of the hall separated from their attendants by a leather curtain or a movable wooden screen or else there was a room behind the High Table, known as the solar, which was their private apartment and could thus contain a permanent bed. A desire for some personal privacy was just beginning to emerge.

At the end of the visit all their belongings were packed up and sent on to the next stop and the house was left an empty shell.

By 1194 Roger de Stuteville was dead as was his only son Anselm who left no children. Though lords of Burton Agnes for only a short time the Stutevilles' manor house remains a substantial and lasting memorial.

The Merleys and the Village

On the death of Anselm de Stuteville his five sisters jointly inherited his estates. The Burton Agnes property came to the Merley family through his sister Alice, wife of Roger de Merley, though not without a family quarrel as another sister, Agnes, (perhaps a possibility for the origin of the name) and her husband Herbert de St. Quintin also claimed it. The Merleys lasted three generations until Alice's grandson, yet another Roger, died leaving only daughters.

There is enough written evidence still in existence to give us a glimpse of life in the village during Roger's ownership. The ravages of William the Conquerer were now nearly two hundred years into history and Burton Agnes had developed into a large and busy rural community. At this time the small village houses clustered around the crossroads whilst up on its hill the Hall, and its occupants, dominated both the scene and the lives of the people.

The struggle to provide enough food to live on while fulfilling their obligations to Roger, and not falling foul of him, left little time or energy for anything else. The land belonging to the village consisted of arable on the hillside to the north of the main road and pasture, fen, and uncultivated moor together with a stretch of water, the mere, on the lowland to the south. Everyone, including Roger, had scattered strips of ploughland in the village's three large communal fields, West, Middle and East; this 'three field system' of agriculture had been introduced by the Saxons and, with local variations, was usual throughout the Midlands and eastern England right up to the eighteenth century and beyond. Each year two of the fields grew crops while the other was left for the soil to recover fertility, helped by allowing cattle to graze on what grew naturally. Roger's tenants were obliged to work his strips as well as their own so in the Spring each of them had to devote two days to ploughing his land and then three days for harrowing. In Autumn they had to harvest for 14 days and, using two carts, spend one day carrying his corn into his storesheds.

After harvest the village's corn was milled as required to turn it into flour for making bread, the basic food for ordinary people. Burton Agnes had two mills, one driven by wind and one by water. The latter was by the stream fed from the springs and was naturally called, as it is today, Mill Beck. By this time the boggy land where the springs emerged had been dug out to form a village pond and this helped to regulate the water driving the mill. Both mills belonged to the Lord of the Manor and tenants had to take their corn to one or the other; this monopoly was much resented and millers, who made their cut on top of the rent they paid to the Lord, were famously the most unpopular members of a village community.

At Christmas each tenant was expected to provide two chickens for the jollifications up at the Hall and their final obligation was the payment of an annual money rent of 4s.6d.

However there were some breaks in the monotony, for Burton Agnes had a market every Tuesday where various everyday necessities were sold including surplus vegetables which people grew in the small gardens attached to their cottages. This contributed to the prosperity of the place and also to that of the lord of the manor as everyone coming from outside to sell paid him a tax. In 1257 the king, Henry III, granted Roger the right to hold a yearly week-long fair at Burton Agnes beginning on November 10th, when merchants from quite far away came bringing goods like ready-made clothing material for those who could afford it. These merchants likewise paid a tax to Roger. From the villagers' point of view probably the best things about the fair were the entertainers who accompanied the merchants and brought a bit of excitement to village life just before the onset of winter. It was needed — the life of the average person in medieval England had not much to recommend it. Modern annual fairs like Hull Fair, held each October, have lost their original purpose and become solely for amusement.

Each village had a constable appointed, often unwillingly, at the manor court and it was his responsibility to bring his miscreant neighbours to the court for a hearing and punishment. In the absence of anything like a modern judicial system lords of the larger manors such as Burton Agnes had permission from the king to enforce summary justice in varying degrees. Thus the village had its own gallows, pillory and tumbril, the latter being a cart which tipped its occupant into the pond, a fairly common sort of punishment. Justice was often swift and rough. The body left hanging and the person vainly attempting to evade missiles in the pillory were salutary warnings to the rest of the population. When merely a fine was called for the lord collected the money. This was the punishment for bakers and brewers who sold underweight or poor quality and was meted out at the Assize of Bread and Ale.

The Somervilles of Wychnor: The Bacon and the Rose

When Roger Merley died in 1265 his property was divided between his daughters Mary and Isabel. His will specified that part of the manor of Burton Agnes should go to each but the sisters came to a more satisfactory arrangement swapping land so that Isabel acquired it all apart from a few acres in Thornholme which went to the Constables of Wassand, who sold it back in 1617.

Isabel's husband, her second, (rich widows were very desirable), was Robert de Somerville and so Burton Agnes became part of his large estate. In 1066 Robert's ancestor Walter de Somerville had left the family home at Evreux in Normandy to fight for his lord William in his conquest of England. Walter was rewarded with a great deal of land including the manor of Alrewas in Staffordshire, formerly belonging to Edwyn, Earl of Mercia, who had staged a rebellion similar to that of Morcar's in Northumberland, and had met a similar fate. Walter built himself a house at Wychnor, a part of his new holding, which is now a tiny village on the bank of the River Trent, just off the A38 south of Burton-on-Trent.

By this time the system of military service in exchange for land, though theoretically still the rule, had in practice given way to a variety of complicated and quite often whimsical arrangements. Robert de Somerville's heirs were his three sons Edmund, Roger and Philip; Edmund, unusually for an eldest son, was a 'magister', a clergyman, and he passed the whole of the Staffordshire property to brother Philip in exchange for £2,000. At this time the manor of Wychnor was held 'by Service of the Bacon'; Philip had to present a side of pork to any married couple that could claim to have lived together without discord for a year and a day, in exactly the same way that the Dunmow Flitch is presented to this day.

Burton Agnes was inherited by Roger, the middle brother, but in later life, though he kept the manor house for himself, he made over the land to his son John for an annual rent of £100 during Roger's lifetime and 'thereafter a rose yearly' to his heirs, Philip and his family.

An example in another family of an unusual and charming rent was that paid by Henry Percy who was given the manor of Leconfield, north of Beverley, by his brother-in-law Peter de Brus on condition that every Christmas Day he should lead Peter's wife by the arm from her chamber to the chapel in Skelton Castle. The Percys went on to build a large house in Leconfield and then spent Christmas there. Only the dried-up moat at Leconfield Castle remains today but a little bit of the house is perhaps incorporated into Burton Agnes Hall as we shall see later.

15

Both Roger and Philip de Somerville were great men; Roger was, as it says on his memorial tablet in Burton Agnes church, 'summoned to Parliament among the Barons of the realm in the 18th (year) of Edward III' (1345) and was Sheriff of Yorkshire while Philip was a member of the Parliament of 1337 and was Sheriff of both Buckingham and Bedford. Parliaments of those times bore no resemblance to today's. Government was by the monarch assisted by his or her Council made up for the most part of close and trusted friends and favourites. The monarch was also expected to run the country and live 'of his own', that is from the proceeds of his own property but from time to time events occurred that needed money from his subjects by way of taxes and at such times he would call a Parliament so that matters could be arranged; the main concern of the members was to protect their own interests from any unwarrantable interference from the king and his ministers, as defined by Magna Carta in 1215.

While power as an MP was thus very limited to be one was indicative of one's power elsewhere and it is interesting that both the Somervilles chose to be buried at Burton Agnes indicating perhaps that it had become the centre of their operations. Roger died in 1337 and Philip in 1354.

Shires and Sheriffs

As can be seen already many of the lords of Burton Agnes occupied the office of Sheriff, a position which still exists. By the time of the Somervilles it was already an ancient office having been introduced by the Saxons when the shires were formed. In 1992 one thousand years of the shrievalty were celebrated. The name is a corruption of 'shire reeve', reeve being a steward or bailiff appointed to oversee the property of his lord. In the case of the Sheriff, his lord was the king, and thus he was the king's chief agent in local government. In the 11th and 12th centuries his powers were considerable; he judged cases in court, could raise the Hue and Cry in his shire (the pursuit of offenders), could summon and command the 'posse comitalis' (the shire's fighting force), was in charge of crown property within the shire and responsible for the collection of all the taxes due to the monarch. Any money that he failed to collect he had to make up from his own pocket and so one might have thought the appointment was a doubtful honour, but in practice it was, certainly to begin with, a lucrative one for which men were ready to offer large sums. Roger de Stuteville's brother William had paid £1,000 for York in 1201. It was lucrative because Sheriffs extorted more money than was due and thus made a profit out of the position. Frequently much disliked — think of the Sheriff of Nottingham in the time of Robin Hood — they were usually too powerful for that to cause them any concern.

Gradually the power of the Sheriffs was eroded: Henry I organised the Exchequer to take over tax collection, Henry II introduced the system of circuit judges from which evolved the Assizes though the Sheriff was still responsible for issuing writs, having ready the court, prisoners and juries and for ensuring the safety and comfort of the judges. Edward I created Commissioners of Array responsible for raising forces and the Tudors introduced Lords Lieutenant as the personal representative of the sovereign.

Between 1856 and 1887 all powers regarding the police and prisons passed to the Prison Commissioners and the Local Constabulary and the Crown Commissioners took over the care of the remaining Crown property. Finally in 1971 Circuit Court Administrators took over responsibility for juries, prisoners and the lodging and transport of county Judges.

So what is left for the modern Sheriff to do? Though he is still technically responsible for the serving of most High Court writs this is done by the under-sheriff, a civil servant, and so the office has become largely ceremonial, a way of recognising some well-known man in the county community who is thought to be a good chap. The Sheriff is still directly appointed by the sovereign and takes office by making a declaration of loyalty; he is second to the Lord Lieutenant in order of precedence and is socially prominent but his official business is now usually restricted to attendance at court with the High Court Judge.

CHAPTER THREE
THE MANOR HOUSE 1341 — 1600

The Griffiths

In 1341 Philip de Somerville signed a document naming his daughter Joan as heir to his Staffordshire and Burton Agnes estates. In 1325 she had married Rhys ap Gruffydd, (pronounced, and later written, Griffith), and thus began that family's ownership of the manor which lasted for over three hundred years culminating in the building of the magnificent Jacobean house which stands there today.

The Griffiths were probably descendants of Rhys ap Gruffydd the last king of Deheubarth, the kingdom of south west Wales, who died in 1170. On his death his kingdom disintegrated amid the quarrels of his sons, one founding a line that eventually settled over the border in Staffordshire. They seem to have carried on being hot-headed and rumbustious, at least in the early generations, though as all we know of them apart from bare facts of births, marriages, deaths, and offices held, consists largely of their appearance in court records this may be an unfair conclusion and probably they were no more belligerent than their contemporaries of similar status.

Rhys ap Gruffydd was certainly a fighting man. We are now in the long reign of Edward III much of which was spent in what turned out to be a vain attempt to conquer France which he claimed through his mother Isabella, a French princess. But there were some famous victories along the way and in 1347 Joan's husband raised an army of 1,000 Welshmen whom he led as their captain via Winchelsea and Calais to join the king at Crécy where the great battle was fought and won. He and his men then stayed in France until the king returned to England and Joan's lot was thus that of many wives — left at home to look after things for long stretches of time while their husbands were away taking part in what is now known as the Hundred Years war.

Rhys ap Gruffydd's roots were clearly still in the land of his fathers, many miles away from Burton Agnes, and his next four descendants seem not to have spent much time there either. This is not to say they took no interest in the place; land was money and power and while the Griffiths may have left much of the day to day running of the estate to their stewards the annual audit would be scrutinised most carefully.

This was often the occasion for a visit by the lord of the manor and his family and just as in the time of Roger de Stuteville, nearly two centuries earlier, all the equipment necessary to the public and highly ritualised lifestyle of the medieval lord came and went with him, only now there was much more since it is highly improbable that the Griffiths, and indeed the Stutevilles before them, in the middle of the 14th century, would take up residence in a one-up-one-down house. At the least a pantry for the bread and a buttery where the butler looked after the wine and ale must have been added somewhere near the kitchen and at the other end of the complex separate chambers for Rhys and his family with perhaps guest lodgings as well.

Dinner remained the most important daily event and was served with great ceremony to the lord as he sat at the high table in the hall with his family and important guests to either side. As the lord's food was carried to him there may have been a trumpet fanfare and his household stood up and took their hats off to honour it. All this pomp was designed to reinforce his position at the head of his particular feudal pyramid and was observed with varying degrees of ostentation from the king downwards.

Rhys II succeeded his father in 1359, having survived the Black Death ten years earlier, when perhaps a third of the country's population died, and went to the war with the Prince of Wales. He was succeeded by his son Thomas who was High Sheriff of Staffordshire in 1430 and was buried at Alrewas. There is more information about John, the next one. Though he was made Sheriff of Staffordshire in 1446 this did not inhibit his behaviour for we find the King's Forester of Alrewas complaining to the Chancellor of England —

"how that Sir John Griffith, which is a common hunter and destroyer of the King's Game, in despite, shame and reproof of the said suppliant, brake (into) the Kynges parke of Barton and there slew and carried away by nyghte tyme two grete buckes and the hedes of them set at Kynges Bromley, own upon the gate of the said forest and another upon the butte in myddes of the town with a scornful scripture of ryme wrytten in Inglish sowed in the mouthes of the bucks hedes."

The Forester protested to Sir John but he

"sent his servants with evil intent to have slayne the said suppliant, who prays for the suerte of the pees in salvation of his lyfe."

How one wishes that the scurrilous verses had survived. In fairness to John it must be said that the exclusion of local people from the king's many hunting parks was a common cause of discontent and he was probably only doing what many of his contemporaries did, or would have liked to do if they could have got away with it.

John's servants appear to have taken their cue from their master for one John Huberd complained that they came to his home at Alrewas and there had

"broken up his dores and turned out his Wyffe and his children stark naked as they were born an taken the dores and solyd them and told the suppliant that if he had been there he would have smote of his hede."

His son Walter was likewise happy to join in any trouble-making for

"with others and his father's servants tried to kill Thomas Nevowe of Ridware while he was making hay at Houndsacre."

Sir Walter Griffith and the Wars of the Roses

In 1455 the Wars of the Roses, the civil war between rival contenders for the crown, the Dukes of Lancaster and York, broke out. The Griffiths' estate in

19

Staffordshire was Duchy of Lancaster property and the Griffith men, John and his sons Walter and John followed their lord into battle. In true family fashion the young men are recorded as being members of a party that attacked and harassed householders while campaigning near London though they appear to have escaped punishment.

Walter is more happily remembered as the man who modernised the manor house at Burton Agnes the oldest part of which had now been standing for some three hundred years. For a long time there had been a movement among land-owners to consolidate their several scattered estates into fewer more easily managed areas by exchange, buying and selling or useful marriage and it became the custom for the eldest son, when he married, to set up his own household in one of his father's subsidiary estates. In 1457 Walter's father leased Burton Agnes to him. Walter raised the walls of the ancient hall and put in a new arch-braced collar-beam roof which is still there; in the west wall he inserted a fine new window with fashionable perpendicular tracery, remnants of which remain.

The other alterations and new building he found necessary for the lifestyle of a well-to-do 15th century lord of the manor we can only guess at. The private chamber had always been general purpose living quarters for besides the bed, the most important piece of furniture and the one which remained ready for use until taken apart for transportation, there was a trestle and board table and stools or chairs for informal meals. Over the last century the homogeneous nature of the occupants of the manor house had broken down and it was increasingly the custom for the lord to eat in state apart from his household in his Great Chamber. As this was usually on the first floor a ceremonial way from the kitchen, through the hall and up the stairs developed, or if as at Burton Agnes the hall was already on the first floor, up the stairs and through the hall.

The presence of some of the surmised accommodation is confirmed in the will of Walter's second wife, Agnes Constable of Flamborough, as she leaves to her son, also Walter,

> "all hangynges of chambers, hall and parlour and all leides, and vessels etc.
> and other stuff I had when I kept house there."

Landowners were always very touchy about possible annexations of bordering land by their neighbours. One of the many small stretches of water — meres — which were a feature of the Holderness landscape before they were drained formed part of the boundary between Walter Griffith's property and that of his neighbour to the south east, Martin de le See of Barmston. Both claimed 'Twenty-fete' near Ulrome Grange and went to law while their tenants, egged on by and sometimes including their lord, engaged in a series of aggravations which left several people injured. Sporadic skirmishing went on through much of 1466, the most serious incident occurring in January when a gang of Walter's men went to Bridlington Priory to lay in wait for Roger Gamesby, servant of Martin de la See, and Thomas Beke struck him dead with his sword.

The documents detailing the end of this dispute are not now to be found but one the previous year with another neighbour, John St. Quintin of Harpham, came to a peaceful conclusion. The moor which formed part of the common lands of Burton Agnes and the neighbouring village of Harpham was very valuable to their economy. Not only were animals grazed there but wild animals and fowl might be captured for the pot and peat was dug out for the fire. The two villages had long been accustomed to sharing the moor but quarrels could and did break out. Eventually Walter and John had a formal agreement drawn up which defined the situation legally. Despite — or perhaps because of? — all this he was thought a suitable person to be appointed Sheriff of Staffordshire in 1473 having come into his inheritance there on the death of his father two years previously.

In her will Agnes Griffith also directed that she should

> *"be buried in Anesburton church in the chauntre closett therein, by Our Lady, as my sonne knowthe,"*

and though she went on to remarry her body was returned to Burton Agnes and rests there as do those of Walter and his first wife Jane (or Joan) Neville. There is a very fine monument to Walter and Jane both of them wearing the metal collar made of reversed SS links which was the emblem of Lancastrians. Jane was entitled to it in her own right as the great-granddaughter of John of Gaunt, Duke of Lancaster. Today some visitors find it strange to see this couple in a Yorkshire church perhaps thinking that the Wars of the Roses were the rather fiercer medieval equivalent of a County cricket match.

Walter died in 1481 when his son, also Walter, was only eight. Technically the heir now became a ward of the monarch until he came of age at 21. In practice what happened was that wardships were sold to someone who then managed the estate for profit and could also arrange the marriage of the ward which gave him the opportunity to settle a poorer female of his own family advantageously. The system was abolished under Cromwell but not before Charles I had used it as a money-making exercise to such an extent that the whole of feudal society was alarmed and the death of an owner while his heir was under age could financially cripple a family. Walter II is yet another of whom very little is known, though he was clearly a man of importance. He married Jane Ferrers of Tamworth, was made a Knight of the Bath, became High Sheriff of Yorkshire in 1501 and was Constable of Scarborough Castle at the time of his death in 1531.

Sir George Griffith

After Walter it is likely that the Griffiths based themselves in Staffordshire again. Where they chose to be buried is always a good clue and his son George's body lies in the church at Tatenhill, the parish church of Wychnor. George was nevertheless eager to add to his Yorkshire estate buying the manor of Little Kelk when it came up for sale in 1549.

Like his forefathers George was knighted as a young man, for him the occasion was in Calais when he was part of the retinue of Henry VIII and Queen Anne Boleyn at their meeting with Francis I of France on the romantically named 'Field of the Cloth of Gold'.

He was also made a Justice of the Peace.

Memorials in Burton Agnes church: foreground, tomb of Sir Walter Griffith (d.1481) and his first wife Jane Neville: on wall, left, memorial tablets to (above) Sir Henry Griffith (d.1620) and (below) Sir Roger (d.1377) and Sir Philip (d.1354) Somerville: right memorial to Sir Henry Griffith Bt. (d.1654) and his first two wives.
Photographs by kind permission of the Rev. D. S. Hawkins, Rector of Burton Agnes.

Sir Walter Griffith III

Even less is known about George's son Walter. He married Katherine Blount, died in 1574 and was buried at Tatenhill. At present therefore his main claim to fame is that he was the father of his son.

Sir Henry Griffith

Henry Griffith was still a minor when his father died and so, like his great-grandfather, became a ward of the monarch, now Queen Elizabeth I. On May 20th 1578 James Croft, the comptroller of the Queen's household acknowledged the receipt of £1,000 from Thomas, Lord Paget of Beaudeserte for the wardship and custody of Henry Griffith Esq. of Wychnor. Henry survived his wardship unmarried and the estate remained intact.

His eventual bride was Elizabeth Throckmorton, (Alrewas parish register spells it Frogmorton), the daughter of Thomas Throckmorton of Coughton, Warwickshire. However the marriage, on February 18th 1584, took place neither at Coughton nor at Wychnor but in Wimbledon. Under the Tudors and especially during the reign of Elizabeth I the country became peaceful. Quarrels were settled by going to law instead of war; the power of the monarch increased and the barons, the largest landowners, found that no longer could they do as they pleased without reference to the central government. Important families concluded that it was economically and socially more useful to be near the court and if possible have a position there. Thus many had a base in or near the capital and presumably their number included the Griffiths and the Throckmortons. However as the latter was the family that plotted against the Queen the previous year one would like to know more about this marriage.

At the same time the court went on lengthy progresses during the summer, the Queen, in the interests of her own housekeeping purse, parking herself and her vast household on favoured subjects who all but bankrupted themselves providing suitable accommodation and entertainment for her, often building completely new houses in the hope, sometimes vain, of a visit. A happy by-product of all this expenditure was the fact that they had no spare money to stage rebellions.

Elizabeth never ventured too far from London and Wychnor was probably just out of her orbit, but a building fever had hit England and Henry Griffith was not immune. In the August following his marriage he started on a new house on an island in the River Trent at Wychnor. Alrewas Parish Register, which is an invaluable source of information having various bits of news inserted into it besides the records of baptisms, marriages and deaths, puts it thus —

"This yeare 1584, the fifth daye of August, was the house at the Trent Yeat Buylded, or as we say begonne to be reared, which house was Buylded by Henry Gryffeth, Esquire."

The register goes on to record

"and the same yeare at the feast of the Nativitie of St. John Baptiste before (June 24th) was the same Henry Gryffeth made one of the Justices for Peace within the County of Stafford."

The Gentry

As the nobility concentrated more and more on their position at court the social rank immediately below them, the territorial descendants of the Norman knights, had been gradually growing in local importance. This was the station in the life of the Griffiths; they were members of 'the gentry', most of whom were still knighted as young men by the sovereign on some suitable occasion, as their fathers and forefathers had been before them, though it was now a social rather than a military distinction.

A contemporary chronicler, Sir Thomas Wilson, writing about the state of England in 1600, counted the nobility as 19 earls, 39 barons and 2 viscounts. He then went on to divide the gentry into knights, about 500, and then those gentlemen 'whose ancestors are or have been knights or else they are the heirs and eldest of their houses'.

The gentry's sphere of influence was the county, for increasingly county administration was being taken into the hands of the J.Ps. who were appointed from its leading members like Henry Griffith, with his large estates in Staffordshire and Yorkshire. Justices might sit on their own or in pairs or informal groups, and every three months the Quarter Sessions were held. Besides administering the law, they set wages and prices, looked after roads and drains, apprenticeships and the relief of poverty, all the things that were eventually taken over by County Councils when they were set up in 1889. But until then the Justices effectively ran the county and it became a matter of pride to be appointed. For some gentlemen that was largely the end of it as apparently one could do as little or as much work as one felt inclined but the Staffordshire Court Records show Henry Griffith as an assiduous and hard-working JP.

Though now far less important than when the office was introduced a Sheriff still had considerable obligations — and expenses — if he was to carry out his duties in a fitting manner: indeed some men tried to avoid it for this reason despite the influence and social prestige it conferred. Not so Henry Griffith who was appointed Sheriff of Staffordshire in 1584.

From all this we can perhaps begin to build a picture of the man: out of a different mould from his belligerent, troublesome ancestors, still very much conscious of his position; welcoming advancement, but earning it through character and application as well as by right of wealth.

As power became centralised into the hands of the monarch and his/her council it became apparent that there was too much work and so in 1536 the Council of the North, having met occasionally in earlier times, was established permanently in York and governed the counties of Yorkshire, Durham, Northumberland, Cumberland and Westmorland. To be a member of the Council was highly sought-after, for the office marked a man out as one held in particular esteem and moreover there was money to be made from it. Staffordshire was not under the Council's jurisdiction but it was perhaps because of his prominence in that county as well as his estate in Yorkshire that Henry Griffith became a member in 1598.

CHAPTER FOUR
THE NEW MANOR HOUSE AT BURTON AGNES, 1600

Planning and Building

It is reasonable to surmise that it was his appointment to the Council of the North that decided Henry to build a new house on his Yorkshire manor of Burton Agnes. It is certain that it brought him the funds to do so for his fortune was now made. He may of course have been bitten by the building bug like so many of his contemporaries and having completed Wychnor decided to start again. Or were the Griffiths looking for a change of luck in their personal lives? With a family name stretching back into the mists of time Henry would naturally be anxious for an heir. Documentary evidence of Henry's family is tantalisingly slight and confusing — he may have had a son Walter and a daughter Margaret by this time, but certainly a son Ralph had died in 1592.

Whatever the reason, at the beginning of 1598 the Griffiths were living in the old manor house at Burton Agnes, a new baby was on the way and building plans were being drawn up. The baby was born on February 10th, a girl, Frances, but still a cause for joy for within two days the news had arrived at Wychnor and been entered in the Alrewas parish register.

As Sir Henry Griffith contemplated the construction of another new house what were his requirements? Accommodation for himself, his family and his servants of course, and all the domestic offices necessary for the maintenance of a highly ceremonial lifestyle; accommodation for travellers of all ranks from the message-bearing servant of a colleague who required a meal and a bed for the night to, he hoped, the highest in the land who might honour him with a visit — all this was essential but the house had to be much more than a place to live in and entertain in. By its appearance, the number and size of its rooms and their decoration it had to be the visible expression of the status and power of a man of position and wealth, a man whose word was law in his own manors, who administered the law in his county and whose importance had been confirmed by his appointment to the Council of the North.

We have seen how the basic hall of the manor house had for centuries been sprouting rooms at both ends, either added on piecemeal to existing buildings or built at one go. This gave a very irregular outline, the function of each component being readily apparent from its appearance, be it the two-storeyed hall with its impressive oriel window at the lord's end or the almost equally impressive kitchen crowned by its louvre designed to create a draught for the vast fireplaces and draw the smoke upwards and out. Though we now find such buildings delightfully romantic, to the first Elizabethans they were merely old-fashioned and out of date. A compact building with a symmetrical facade was now the imperative, but behind that the basic layout remained the same which could give rise to some strange planning contortions. Sir Henry Griffith

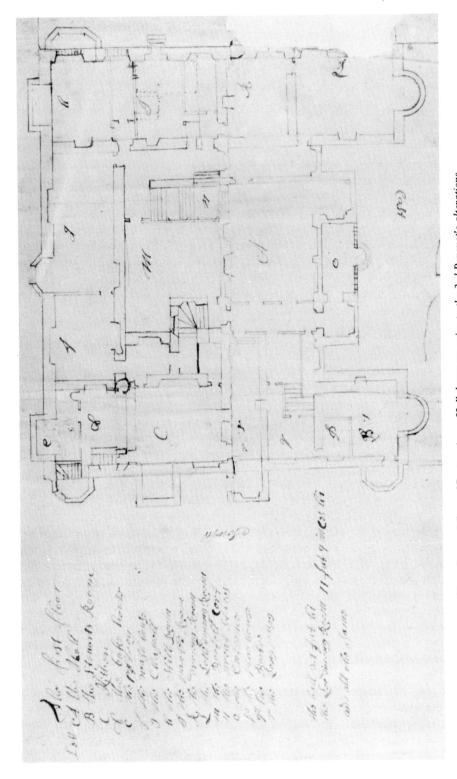

Plan of ground floor of Burton Agnes Hall drawn up prior to the 3rd Baronet's alterations.

26

cannot have failed to be aware of two houses recently built only a short detour from his route between Wychnor and Burton Agnes, Wollaton Hall, begun in 1580 and Hardwick Hall built between 1591 and 1597. In both of them one of the main problems was solved by placing the Great Hall at right angles to the main front instead of along it but this could not prevent Hardwick, 'more glass than wall' having some of its magnificent windows giving on to the backs of chimneys or having floors built across them.

As he was building himself it is not too fanciful to think that he must have watched them rise up with above average interest, making it more than a coincidence that, though not quite in the same league as the formidable and flamboyant Countess of Shrewsbury, 'Bess of Hardwick', for Burton Agnes he employed the same architect, Robert Smythson, master-mason to the Queen.

The Burton Agnes ground plan reverted to an earlier solution where the rooms previously stretching out at either end of the Great Hall were wrapped round an internal courtyard with, in this case, the chapel, used both by family and household forming the join. With great ingenuity all the rooms had windows properly placed, the most important having the new bay ones, either square, angled or 'compass' (semi-circular), a 'first' for Burton Agnes, that form such an attractive feature of the elevations.

The material used was brick probably made from local clay in brickyards set up in the village. Though the Romans had built their villas and some town walls of brick — there is still a substantial section of Roman brick wall at York — when they left the native population and their new invaders reverted back to timber and mud where stone was not available or too expensive and it was not until the 13th century that bricks were again manufactured. Roger de Stuteville, who was rich, built the Norman manor house of stone but later additions had been of brick. Henry would use stone for the plinth, quoins, window frames, mullions and transoms, to emphasise the front door and to decorate the facade.

Naturally, succeeding generations have modernised and adapted the house to take account of fashion and to suit their own requirements though there was never enough money to make wholesale alterations. Nevertheless some detective work is necessary to envisage the house as it was when first completed. Luckily we have two valuable clues; first an account of a tour of the house made by the famous traveller and diarist Celia Fiennes when she visited her cousin Sir Griffith Boynton in 1697 before the alterations which he made and secondly a sketch plan probably drawn by or for him of the ground floor of the house, perhaps to help him plan the new works. This last was found in the house by John Bilson early this century and is now lost but fortunately was reproduced in the Yorkshire Archaeological Journal Volume 21 1910.

A Visit to Burton Agnes Hall

There is a tradition that King James VI of Scotland stayed at Burton Agnes in 1603 on his way to Westminster to be crowned simultaneously James I of England on the death of Elizabeth I. Since the dates 1601 appear above the front door and 1602 and 1603 in the rainwater heads of the west and east wings respectively it would seem that the house was still under construction at that time and that such a visit is highly unlikely. In any case it is not documented in the account of the royal progress. However Henry Griffith provided a State Guest Apartment of some splendour, perhaps in hopes of such a visit in the future: Burton Agnes, though some distance off the direct route of the Great North Road, is almost exactly halfway between London and Edinburgh and might have made a handy stopping place had the king taken to commuting between the two capitals. Unfortunately he did not. However we can assume that people of high rank did stay in the house and we can get some idea of it at that time if we follow such a person on his first visit.

It is likely that Sir Henry rode out to meet his guest and the accompanying members of his household to escort him the last few miles of his journey; this would give Henry the opportunity to point out early glimpses of his house which, standing on the first rise of the Yorkshire Wolds, was visible from some distance. Round it was a high brick wall broken at the front by the gatehouse built in the same style as the house but with four turrets surmounted by lead cupolas at its corners. A gatehouse had been the first line of defence in previous troubled times but now its purpose was to provide an imposing entrance. The horsemen passed under the central archway, tactfully surmounted by a large carved stone coat-of-arms of James I, and into the formal gardens laid out in front of the house. In the middle was a bowling green enclosed by a fence and the approach to the house went round it. As we know from the story of Sir Francis Drake bowls was a very popular game at this time. The front door then, as now, is not at all obvious being as Celia Fiennes described it 'in the side of the tower which was the old fashion in Building'. This positioning was a playful touch, a 'device', much beloved at the time whether in architecture, garden design or riddles.

Having dismounted and handed their horses over to the grooms to be taken to the stables the party entered the house by way of a small lobby into the 'Screens Passage'. On the left were the traditional three arches leading to the kitchen, buttery, pantry and all the other service rooms and on the right two rather larger arches led through the Screen to the Great Hall. In ancient manor houses movable wooden screens had been placed in front of the doors leading to the outside and the kitchen as some protection against draughts and smells; over the years they joined up and became a sort of false wall, but still called the Screen.

The layout of the house was very familiar to the new arrival — his own and every other house he went to was more or less the same — so he walked through one of the arches into the Great Hall to be formally greeted by his host and hostess while his servants waited with his travelling bags. But he would be curious to see how Sir Henry had stamped his personality (and evidence of his wealth) on this two-storey high room, the hub of his house and the place where first impressions were made.

The High Table was in its usual position at the far end lit by the square bay window which balanced the entrance lobby and the walls were panelled in the usual oak, but the carving was exceptionally fine as it was throughout the house. Above the fireplace was a splendid alabaster relief of the Bible story of the wise and foolish virgins. If the visitor looked behind him he could not have failed to be struck by the appearance of the Screen, there seems not to have been another one quite like it anywhere else. The usual arrangement was to build it about 10 feet high with quite often a low ceiling to the Screens Passage behind forming

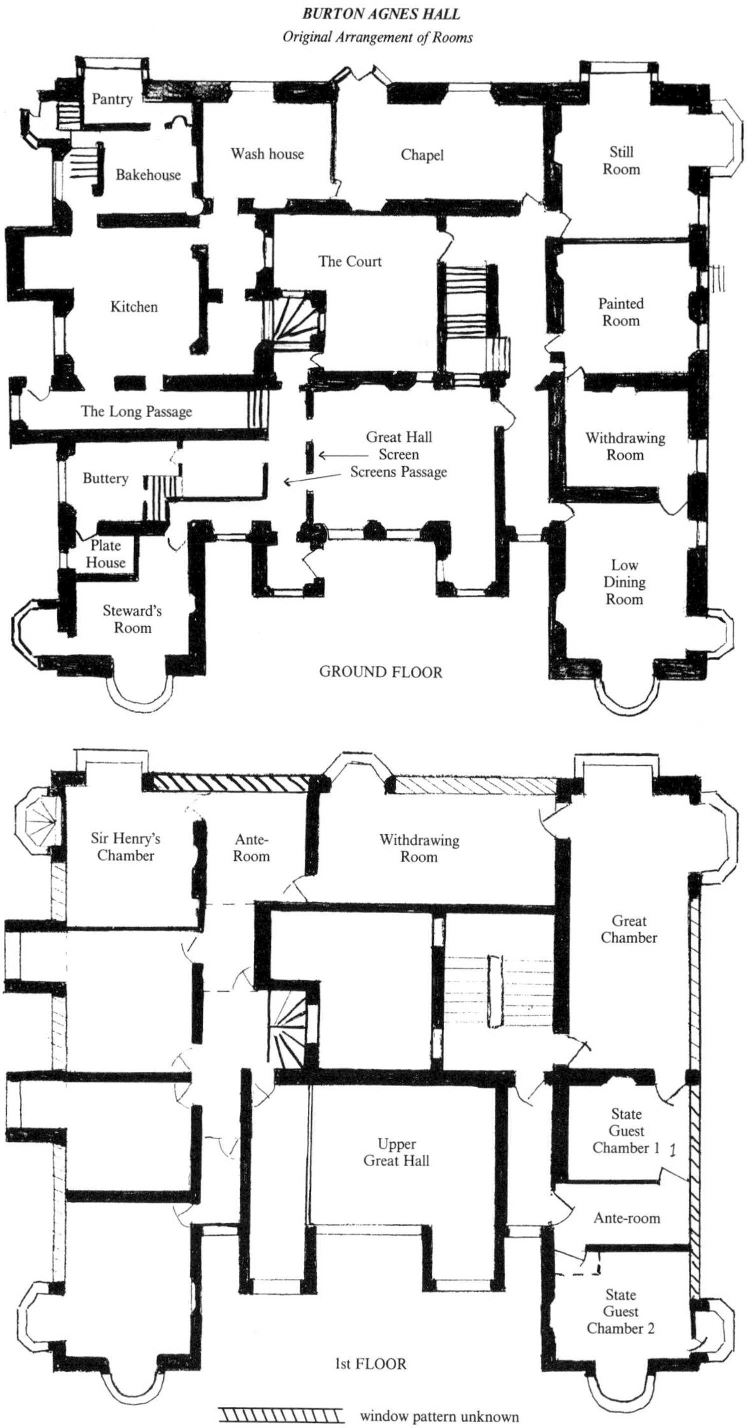

BURTON AGNES HALL
Original Arrangement of Rooms
Pantry
Bakehouse
Wash house
Chapel
Still Room
The Court
Kitchen
Painted Room
The Long Passage
Great Hall
Screen
Screens Passage
Withdrawing Room
Buttery
Plate House
Low Dining Room
Steward's Room
GROUND FLOOR
Sir Henry's Chamber
Ante-Room
Withdrawing Room
Great Chamber
Upper Great Hall
State Guest Chamber 1
Ante-room
State Guest Chamber 2
1st FLOOR
window pattern unknown

Burton Agnes Hall: above, original arrangement of ground floor; below, surmised original arrangement of first floor.

The principal staircase made of oak. The wall panelling is 18th century mahogany.

the floor to a gallery where musicians could play. But at Burton Agnes, above the carved woodwork, a vast superstructure of tiered plaster figures in high relief rises to the ceiling, looking very much like a triumphal arch and indeed bearing some resemblance to those erected in London for the coronation of King James. Could Sir Henry have been present on that occasion? As an educated man of his time the visitor would immediately recognise by their accompanying symbols the four evangelists writing their gospels with above them the 12 apostles, though some what mysteriously here, and through the house, many carved facial features are distorted rather in the manner of Roman 'grotesques'. Below the plasterwork the wooden part of the screen ends in a long panel depicting the twelve sons of Jacob, the founding fathers of the tribes of Israel. Each has an identifying doggerel verse beside him (see page 68) but this can only be read with the aid of a ladder and a torch — how amazing to put so much effort into something that would hardly ever be appreciated. The Screen also contains many classical and allegorical figures whose meanings are no longer readily apparent to us today but would have been then.

The visitor was led up the grand staircase which ascended, as was correct, from the side of the High Table. This was made not of the usual stone but of wood, at the time quite an innovation as joiners had only just become confident of making such a large structure load-bearing and its double newel posts do seem to indicate a belt-and-braces approach to the problem. Be that as it may, the result with all its ornate decoration provided an impressive ceremonial route to the great entertaining rooms on the first floor.

At the head of the stairs a door on the left gave entry to the Great Chamber but probably the visitor would first be shown to his lodgings, the entrance to which lay ahead. This was a self contained suite comprised of a wide passage leading to an ante-room which gave on to two chambers. The principal chamber was got up fit for a king with highly carved oak panelling covering the walls. There was a distinct classical influence in the choice of motifs, the ionic capitals of pilasters supporting a frieze in the form of 'terms' — busts on pedestals —which in turn support the ceiling, with its restrained but decorative geometric plasterwork.

If the visitor's Lady accompanied him (though this was not very usual) she would be shown into the other room, just as ornately decorated and with classical columns flanking the fireplace but generally with a more feminine feel. The doorway had a small internal porch with carvings of St. Judith and St. Barbara above. Panels of leaves with fruit, flowers and berries decorate the wall-panelling. The fireplace surround contains allegorical figures of Patience, Truth, Constancy and Victory and interwovern in the carving above them is the date 12th July 1610, now a mystery but perhaps marking the final completion of the house.

The 'Queen's Room': detail of honeysuckle ceiling.

LIBRARY
BISHOP BURTON COLLEGE
BEVERLEY HU17 8QG

The most beautiful decoration, however, is reserved for the ceiling, an incredibly complicated design of honeysuckle with some of the branches forming hanging loops. It is thought to be unique and therefore very special as most designs for plasterwork and carving were taken from one of the several pattern books in circulation at the time and can be seen repeated in many contemporary houses. Sir Henry must have employed a plasterer who was a master of his craft. In the far corner of the room a door led to a closet or 'cabinet' contained by the angled window where the lady could retire for privacy and where her maid might sleep at night. Their servants would now arrive bearing the luggage and while some unpacked it others attended to their lord and lady after their journey.

Meanwhile the resident household was getting ready for that climax of the day's activities, dinner, served to Sir Henry and his guest in the Great Chamber. As we have noted previously this room had for a long time taken on function of the medieval Great Hall for state occasions and in many ways its layout was the same though with even more splendidly decorated walls and ceiling. The High Table was again placed across the room at the end furthest from the door and at Burton Agnes there is an angled bay window giving it that extra light and distinction that was always a feature of the High Table end of the Great Hall. This window is balanced on the east facade by the similar one that forms the closet in the Queen's room.

Now the table was set for the meal, the diners still sitting at one side only and facing down the room where a trestle table was erected for those who had the honour of eating in the Great Chamber but didn't quite make it to the top table. On an occasion such as we are describing those at the top table were likely to be gentlemen neighbours of Sir Henry, Sir Francis Boynton of Barmston, Sir William Constable of Flamborough, Sir Jon Hotham of Scorborough and perhaps Sir John Constable of Burton Constable (not related to the Flamborough family).

The butler unlocked the Plate House, a strong room with access only from his buttery, and the silverware it contained would be taken up to the Great Chamber and arranged on the side-board to provide a fitting and proper display of wealth. He then brought wine up from the cellar, the steps again leading into the buttery. The bread which accompanied the meal was got from the pantry next to the bakehouse.

Now the activity in the kitchen was reaching its height and the meal, mainly of several kinds of fish, meat, poultry and game — vegetables were very little eaten by the rich and the poor could seldom afford meat — was ready to be served. Sir Henry invited his guest to join him and after host, guest, family and other visitors of rank were seated according to strict rules of precedence, the food and drink began its procession from the kitchen, down the Long Passage, into the Screens Passage, and so into the Great Hall. Here the servants, joined by the visiting ones, were assembled at trestle tables to eat their own food, possibly presided over by the steward though he and the upper members of both households may have eaten in his room. As the food for upstairs was taken through, the Great Hall assembly paid it suitable respect as ever. The procession then mounted the stairs and turned left into the Great Chamber where what must by now have been the rapidly cooling repast was served with the utmost ceremony which even further delayed the actual moment of eating. Hot food was definitely a secondary consideration to the manner in which it was presented.

When the meal was finished Sir Henry invited the company into his Withdrawing Room which was through the door to his right. While they were thus 'withdrawn', the remains of the meal were cleared away and the room prepared for the entertainment that was to follow. Or they may have climbed the stairs to the second storey to take a little exercise in the Gallery which at 115 feet stretched the length of the house. There was great competition among house builders as to the size of a gallery they could contrive and Sir Henry's, in a house of many splendid rooms sumptuously decorated, must surely have been his pride and joy for not only was it long but the beautiful barrel ceiling with its realistically painted plaster flowers and foliage, some of the leaves hanging from their branches, gave one the impression of walking through a bower. Here, on the plain oak-panelled walls, were hung portraits of the family, their relations and friends with most likely some royal portraits as well, copies of those made by the court painters. If it was still light Sir Henry could point out the extent of his land through the many windows and on a clear day they might have seen, as did Celia Fiennes, ships under sail in Bridlington Bay, five miles distant. The braver visitor with a head for heights might have climbed the final flight of stairs and gone through the door leading to the roof where he could breathe in the fresh air blowing from the North Sea.

On another day they may have walked in the garden, perhaps along the Crooked Walk described by Celia Fiennes as being

"Of grass well Cutt and rowled, it is indented in and out in Corners, and so in the wall wch makes you thinke you are at the end of the walke Severall tymes before you are, by means of the Codling hedge that is on the other side."

She says the walk leads to a Summer House but it may have been used as a Banqueting House in Sir Henry's time. A banquet then was not what we think of today but rather the final course of the meal eaten either in the Withdrawing Room or in one of these little buildings specially erected for the purpose usually in the garden but occasionally on the roof. These were intimate occasions, not everyone being invited to partake, and the food served might include spiced jellies or fruit in syrup with little sugar and cinnamon cakes or marzipan.

This is the sort of thing that Lady Griffith would have made with her ladies and daughters in her Still Room. At this time the 'pudding' course of the main meal was sweetmeats, literally sweet meat. Blancmange for instance, 'white food' was made from the pale flesh of chicken and rabbit, pounded to a paste and mixed with ground almonds, honey and milk. Despite the amazingly elaborate concoctions that issued from them, kitchens were sordid and bloody places where sides of animals were heaved on the spits next to roaring open fires by half naked kitchen boys and they remained much the same for a surprisingly long time. It was no place for banquet food, still less for a lady. All the staff except the laundresses were male at this time.

The Still Room got its name from its other function; Lady Griffith was

Principal State Guest Chamber ('King's Room').

*Fireplace wall of what was probably Sir Henry Griffith's chamber showing chimney-piece
with the four Cardinal Virtues, Prudence, Justice,
Fortitude and Temperance.*

responsible for the health of the household and here the medicines from garden herbs and lightly alcoholic cordials were distilled.

Back in the Great Chamber the party would continue with the entertainment, perhaps dancing or cards until it was time for bed, the guest having direct access to his chamber via a door at the far end of the room which, no doubt, was a great convenience at the end of a convivial evening. Sir Henry and his family could then retire through the Withdrawing Room to their own quarters beyond, the master bedroom, though not as grand as that designed for a king, distinguished by an imposing plasterwork fireplace. One hopes they were filled with satisfaction and perhaps a little relief at the end of a successful day.

As for those other conveniences, the calls of nature were answered by the close stool, a sort of shallow bucket with a lid contained in a low seat with a suitable opening, the whole thing often quite elaborately draped and upholstered. Water closets using rainwater had been installed in earlier houses particularly those with moats into which they discharged but these and the outlets themselves, in the absence of the yet uninvented U-bends and valves, became distinctly malodorous and the close stool, taken away by a servant after use and the contents disposed of in the midden was, for the time being, a more hygienic arrangement.

The guest was now prepared for the night by members of his own staff who themselves slept on straw mattresses or truckle beds in the ante-room so as to be available whatever the hour. All the bedroom doors at Burton Agnes had a clever locking device incorporating a brass weight on the end of a cord which went by means of loops hanging from the ceiling to a handle by the bed. Thus privacy was assured but servants or whoever could be admitted without the necessity of getting out of bed.

The Griffiths would have had between 20 and 30 living-in servants but very little household sleeping accommodation was provided in the new house as the old building was made over for this purpose. The family's closest attendants would sleep in the ante-rooms to their chambers, the Steward in his own room and the lowest ranks such as kitchen boys in an alcove near their work place.

The family

When the visit was over the family went back to eating in the Low Dining room, the first and grandest room in the suite of three family parlours which lay through a door behind the Great Hall high table. Beyond that was the necessary Withdrawing Room, both rooms described by Miss Fiennes as well proportioned,

> *"and the wanscoate* (the oak panelling) *is all well Carv'd, the moulding of the doores and Chimneys are finely Carv'd with Staggs and all sorts of beasts, woods and some leaves and flowers and birds and angells etc."*

She goes on,

> *"There is beyond this a very good little parlour with plaine wanscoate painted in veines like marble, dark and white Streakes."*

Aother 'device' perhaps?

At the end of these rooms came the Still Room; as Elizabeth Griffith's work room it was part of the family area, yet because of the nature of the work it was also, via the courtyard, accessible to the household.

Sir Henry Griffith lived to enjoy his house until 1620 when he died at the good age of 60. On his memorial tablet in the church his children are given as Walter, Ralph and Henry, his heir, Margaret and Frances, but by the time of Norroys Heraldic Visitation of York in 1612 only Henry and Frances are recorded. We know that Ralph died young so presumably the others did also. For a man whose family had a long and distinguished history, and who had built two great houses, all his hopes for the future of his line were thus centred on this one surviving son.

The Burton Agnes Parish Register records the baptism of the young Henry on 7th August 1602, and, as with Frances, the birth was also entered at Alrewas —

"Henry Griffith s. of Henry natus fuit hoc tempore apud Agnes Burton."

No date is given but the entry is between others of 31st July and 5th August. Presumably the boy spent his early years at Burton Agnes and then perhaps went away to school although the custom of sending sons of the gentry to get their education in the households of the aristocracy had not yet entirely died out.

The Marriage of Frances

Though the future of the line must remain in doubt until the heir marries and himself has a son in the meantime Sir Henry had the happiness of seeing his daughter Frances admirably settled, for on 27th September 1614 she married Matthew, the son and sole heir of his late neighbour Francis Boynton of Barmston. The young couple were 16 and 24 respectively and set up home at Roxby, north of Whitby, where the Boyntons had an estate. Though what little evidence we have points to an affectionate union marriages were very much business arrangements between families and this one must have brought considerable satisfaction to both sides. For Henry Griffith he had secured for his only daughter a husband already in possession of his family's considerable property and for the Boyntons, not only did Frances bring an excellent dowry with her, but should the one remaining male Griffith fail to produce heirs there was the agreeable prospect of the amalgamation of two extensive bordering estates together with a large modern house.

There was also the Staffordshire property although Henry had sold a fair amount of this to produce the dowry, to wit:-

70 messuages, 70 cottages, 40 tofts, 3,500 acres of lands (strips on the common fields), 2,500 acres of meadow, 2,000 acres of pasture, 80 acres of wood, 2,500 acres of moor and 70s of rent in Wichnor, Tunstall, Tatenhill, Birdsall, Newbold, Alreywas, Fridley, Ongreve and Edingwall.

For all this he received £3,800, £2,000 of which, together with other land, was settled on Frances. This was an unusually large amount and the fact that Sir Henry was prepared to fork out so much indicates his pleasure at the match.

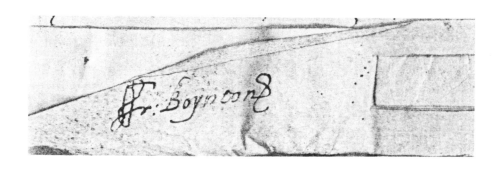

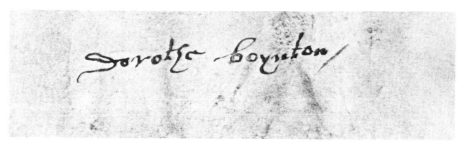

Signatures of Matthew Boynton and his mother, Dorothy, at the foot of the marriage settlement of Matthew and Frances Griffith.

Sir Henry Griffith: An Archetypal English Gentleman of the time.

While Henry was prepared to sell land in Staffordshire he was adding to his Yorkshire estate whenever the opportunity arose and in 1611 he had bought the village of Haisthorpe, a mile from Burton Agnes Hall, which had originally belonged to the Stutevilles and likewise in 1617 the part of nearby Thornholme already mentioned which had been acquired by the Constables of Wassand from the Merleys in 1265. This rounding off of a principal estate is so typical of the time, indeed if one were looking for a textbook member of the successful gentry of the early 17th century Sir Henry Griffith would be the man. By talent and application he rose to one of the top positions in the north of England and thereby became rich. He managed his estate profitably, built his houses and married his daughter well. He enjoyed his wealth and position as was entirely proper but also conscientiously carried out the obligations that went with his privileged status. He was Sheriff of Yorkshire in 1606 and though Burton Agnes was now his main residence he still sat as a magistrate in Staffordshire. He must have been constantly on horseback.

But the real nature of the man we can only guess at. One source says that 'in the north the family were known as the grave Griffiths' and this perhaps ties up with the unusual amount of Biblical carvings which decorate his house. It is true that the Bible dominated all personal behaviour and political thought at this time. It had only become readily available in English translation a generation before and as all truth was thought to be contained in it men searched diligently through the text for answers to the questions of the age. The location of one's afterlife was also a constant preoccupation amongst thinking

The 'Dance of Death' on the Drawing Room chimney-piece showing winged death trampling on symbols of wealth and power with (left) the righteous clustered round sheep and (right) the unrighteous with goats.

people and the exhortations of Jesus that Judgement Day might occur at any time were taken very seriously. thus one must endeavour to be amongst the chosen, the sheep of the Good Shepherd, and so we find the extraordinary carving of the 'Dance of Death' above the fireplace in the Low Dining Room (now the downstairs Drawing Room), with its clear indication that the righteous were going to Heaven and the unrighteous (the goats) to Hell. The wise and foolish virgins carving in the Great Hall carries the same message and there may well have been others in similar vein which are now lost. These views were particularly held by Puritans, a term first used in the time of Elizabeth to denote those who thought the newly-established protestant church had not gone far enough in its stance against 'popery'. Whatever Sir Henry called himself, all the evidence we have, tenuous though it is, leads to a man who endeavoured to conduct his life in what at the time seemed a sober Christian manner with the hope of a place in Heaven at the end of it.

CHAPTER FIVE
SIR HENRY GRIFFITH Bt (1602-1654)

A Royal Visit

If Sir Henry was aware of his approaching death his last days must have been sadly clouded by the bad news that yet again the heir was going into wardship. He had done his best to soften the effects by entailing the estate on future generations but nevertheless a third was leased out until young Henry came of age. There are also some indications that the young man was not turning out entirely as his father might have wished.

Whether by his own desire or by the arrangement of his guardian, Henry was speedily married the following year to Mary, the daughter of Sir Henry Willoughby, and just as his sister and her husband had gone to live at Roxby so Henry and Mary took up residence at Wychnor, though as his father was dead Burton Agnes was available to him.

Thus most of the action, and there is quite a lot of it, now takes place elsewhere. First, that supreme accolade of a Royal visit, long waited for in vain by his father, was almost immediately granted to young Henry for Alrewas parish register records:-

"August 21st 1621 the King at Whichnor and the Court at the Hall there."

Then three years later another visit,

"August 19 1624, the King dyned at Whichnor."

When one was honoured by a visit from the monarch he and his household took over the place entirely. He would sit at the centre of the High Table with his entourage around him, his host being relegated to a subsidiary position elsewhere. King James and his court were well known for rowdy, drunken behaviour at dinner; indeed he has been described as one of the most uncouth kings England ever had and a contemporary, Sir Anthony Weldon, wrote,

"His Tongue (was) *too large for his mouth which ever made him speak full in the mouth, and made him drink very uncomely, as if eating his drink, which came out of the cup of each side of his mouth; His skin was as soft as Taffeta Sarsnet, which felt so because he never washed his hands, only rubbed his finger ends slightly with a wet end of a napkin –."*

By this time the king, at 58, was also showing signs of premature senile dementia, and indeed was within six months of his death, so perhaps the visit was less of a joy than it might have been and Burton Agnes was well off without one. One wonders how Henry and Mary coped and what repairs and replacements were necessary. Yet King James is the man who authorised that great translation of the Bible in 1611 and the author himself of several learned tracts.

39

In the meantime we learn,

"1622 This year the fallowfields of Alrewas were first sowed with pease,"

so Henry, or maybe his steward, was an innovative land user.

But life was far from smooth for Henry Griffith. Some time before 1633 his wife Mary died childless for in that year he married as his second wife Dorothy, the daughter of Sir Henry Bellingham. Tragedy must have again struck and this time swiftly as Henry married for the third and last time on 17th January 1635. His new bride was Margaret Wortley and almost immediately she became pregnant with the long awaited heir, but who, for reasons we can only guess at,

Memorial to Grace Griffith (d.1641) and her infant sister (d.1640) in Tatenhill church, Staffordshire.

was given not a Griffith family name as would have been usual, but his mother's maiden name. Sadly baby Wortley survived only a short time and was buried at Tamworth in 1636. A daughter was born in 1640 but did not even live long enough to be baptised and this was done pretty smartly if the baby looked likely to die so as to enable its soul to enter Heaven. She was buried at Tatenhill in October 1640. Finally another daughter, Grace, was buried also at Tatenhill on 18th December 1641. Grace has a very touching monument in Tatenhill church showing the little girl kneeling in prayer. Its Latin inscription, which remembers also her baby sister, states that it is offered up by Henry Griffith, Baronet, and Lady Margaret, his dearest wife. There were to be no more children and so Henry lived out his life knowing he was the last of his line.

A Royalist in the Civil War

Disappointed and unhappy though he must have been Henry was obliged to give his attention to other matters, for England was gearing itself up to Civil War. The causes were many and complex; even in the time of James a division was growing between the King and Parliament, composed as it was for the most part of decent-living gentry, who objected to paying taxes to support the scandalous goings-on at court. When his son Charles became king in 1625 his foreign policy immediately alienated Parliament which refused to grant him any money at all, not even the customs dues ('tunnage and poundage') usually granted to a king for life at the beginning of his reign. But Charles continued to collect them and after more quarrels with Parliament he dissolved it in 1629 and did not call another until 1640 by which time it was too late to repair the breach. In the meantime, under the protection of Henrietta Maria, Charles' Queen, Roman Catholicism, a supposedly outlawed religion, had become fashionable at court, and religious problems were also causing trouble with Scotland leading to armed conflict. There were yet more horrendous problems in Ireland, and in the end, with petitions from the counties and demonstrations in the towns and the continuing lack of money Charles was forced to give in and Parliament was summoned.

The Short Parliament sat for only three weeks but at the end of the year the Long Parliament which was not to be dissolved for nearly 20 years met and immediately it was obvious that Charles had no control over it whatsoever. Two of his ministers were arrested, one subsequently being executed, and others fled the country. An act was passed saying it could not be dissolved without its own consent. The Speaker, who previously had been appointee of the sovereign's now saw himself quite differently and when Charles came to the House, hoping to arrest five members, Speaker Lenthall famously said to him, "I have neither eyes to see nor tongue to speak in this place, but as the house is pleased to direct me, whose servant I am."

But not all Members of Parliament and the gentry in the counties were happy at the way things were going. Many believed in the Divine Right of Kings and felt they would be breaking God's law by opposing Charles. Others thought, and with reason, that a revolution such as appeared likely might be difficult to stop at the point where they got what they wanted and would spread to the population at large so that the mass of people, their tenants on their estates, who in many cases had good cause to be unhappy at their lot, might rise against them.

So parties were formed by men who, often reluctantly and with great anguish of mind, felt obliged to throw in their lot with one side or the other. There were of course hotheads on both sides, one of whom was Henry Griffith's father-in-law, Sir Francis Wortley, whose action on 3rd May 1642 in drawing his sword and swearing to support the King against Parliament by beginning to raise a troop of 200 horsemen is regarded as the first overt Royalist action. Was it because he was influenced by his wife's family that Henry was also a Royalist? Puritans generally supported Parliament and one has the feeling that old Sir Henry would have done. Certainly his son-in-law Matthew Boynton did.

Meanwhile King Charles had been obliged to leave London and was roaming the country in search of support. In April he had approached Hull with the intention of inspecting the royal arsenal held in the town. But Hull was supporting Parliament and the military governor, Sir John Hotham, after much discussion with the town council, shut the Beverley Gate in the King's face. A slanging match between Sir John, standing on the battlements, and the King, on horseback below, ensued but Sir John would not give way and the King had to withdraw. From this point civil war became inevitable and the first engagement was a drawn battle at Edgehill on 23rd October.

No-one escaped the ravages of the war whether they were in an area like Staffordshire where set-piece battles were fought or the East Riding where Hull was twice besieged and houses of Parliamentarians were sacked by marauding bands of Royalists and vice-versa. Troops were billeted on unwilling houseowners and tenants took advantage of the times to settle old scores. In 1643, desperately looking for money to finance the war, Parliament was sufficiently in charge to order that the estates of Royalists be 'sequestered', that is taken away from their owners, and so the Griffiths found themselves almost landless and their income reduced to the one fifth which they were allowed to retain to maintain themselves.

Margaret may have had to cope with the sequestrators, as many wives did, for their husbands were away fighting. Henry was on active service in King Charles' army and in July 1644 was in the Battle of Marston Moor where the Royalists were soundly defeated and many lives were lost. The war continued with fortune swinging from side to side until Parliament with its New Model Army seized the initiative in 1645 and by June 1646 King Charles had admitted defeat and given himself up. On 30th January 1649 he was executed as a traitor; all that Henry Griffith and his fellow Royalists had fought and suffered for seemed lost for ever.

But now war-weariness and a horror at what was happening to the country combined with considerable apprehension at signs that the tenantry were about to get out of control made people, especially the gentry, long to get back to some form of order and thus, quite early on, sequestered estates were allowed to be bought back, Henry paying the enormous sum of £8,793 for his, and having to sell land in order to raise the money. Eventually some of this was repaid; in what was really a further attempt to mend the fabric of society and allow the gentry to get back on their feet again it was realised that large parts of

estates that had been sequestrated technically belonged not to the present occupant but to future generations by virtue of the entailing system. Making every effort to preserve his property intact for the future generations Henry's father had arranged that only part of it was settled on him for life, the rest was in trust for his wife, then to his first son, other sons and right down the line to the sons of his sister, Lady Boynton.

In this way Henry got back all the Griffith property except that which was legally his to lose.

The End of the Griffiths

Henry Griffith died in 1654. He had bought his baronetcy from King Charles in 1627 but had not been appointed a JP until 1642 when Charles was at York just prior to the start of the war and at the height of it he was unable to exercise his new powers as sessions were suspended in Staffordshire. He had lived through some of the most troubled times in English history. The monarchy had gone, for good for all he knew, and England was ruled by Lord Protector Cromwell. He had buried two wives and three children. He had recovered most of his property but had no direct heir to pass it on to. He had not been a fortunate man.

There is a curiously macabre monument with three coffins on it in Burton Agnes church *"In memory of Sir Henry Griffith and his two wives, the one (as appears by the arms) a Willoughby and the other a Bellingham."* No mention of Margaret Wortley but it is probable that she and Henry are buried in Staffordshire . There is also the memorial tablet to the first Sir Henry already mentioned. The Wychnor house was pulled down in the 18th century but the great house at Burton Agnes remains in all its glory. What else is there to remind us of the proud line of Griffith that ended so soon after its greatest achievements? They must have had many portraits made of themselves, to hang in the Long Gallery and give as presents to their friends in the custom of the day, but the picture of a sweet-faced lady in puritan dress, long thought to be Frances Griffith, on close inspection turns out to be that of someone aged 46. Frances died at 34, and by the heraldry is possibly a member of the West family of Aughton in south Yorkshire. Another large painting labelled 'Frances, Margaret and Catherine Griffith' would be difficult to authenticate. With the marvellous exception of the house there is precious little to remind us of the family today... except, perhaps, the ghost, 'the blue lady' seen by some, her presence felt by others, known in the village as 'Owd Nance', but thought by many to be that of Anne, an unrecorded daughter of the first Sir Henry.

LIBRARY
BISHOP BURTON COLLEGE
BEVERLEY HU17 8QG

CHAPTER SIX
THE BOYNTONS OF BARMSTON

The Early Family

In 1654, at the death without heirs of his uncle Henry Griffith and in accordance with his grandfather's will, Sir Francis Boynton, Bart., of Barmston, already in possession of much property, inherited the Griffith estates making him one of the largest gentry landowners in the north of England. He was now Lord of the manors of Barmston, Burton Agnes, Roxby, Greno and East and West Scaling in Yorkshire and Wychnor in Staffordshire and owned further land in Thornholme, Rudston, Little Kelk, Haisthorpe and Boynton.

It is presumed that the family took its name from the latter village, only a few miles from both Barmston and Burton Agnes, and where they owned land from earliest times. By 1222 Ingleram de Boynton was living at Acklam in what is now the county of Cleveland and it was marriage to an heiress that brought them back to their ancestral homeland.

Like their future relatives, the Griffiths, the Boyntons' history is full of incident, one nearly finishing them off. In 1405 Henry Boynton was one of the many northern landowners who joined in the Percy rebellion against King Henry IV, most of whom lost their lives. Henry Boynton was beheaded in Berwick-upon-Tweed where he had sought refuge when the rebellion collapsed and his head was subsequently delivered to the mayor of Newcastle who in return for displaying it on the town bridge, to be left there as long as the ghastly thing would last, was given all Henry's forfeited property. After a month, however, he was told to deliver the head to Henry's wife for burial. It cannot have been much consolation to the poor lady, widowed and destitute with nothing to support herself and her six children, but in an act of clemency the following August she was given back Roxby and Newton and thus the family survived.

The Boynton village land returned to its namesake in the next generation when William Boynton petitioned the king for its restoration and William's son Thomas provided an annuity for his two sisters out of it.

It was Thomas's son, Henry, who was responsible for the eventual resettlement of the family in East Yorkshire for he married Margaret de la See, daughter and co-heir of that Martin de la See of Barmston with whom Walter Griffith had such a disastrous quarrel. Nevertheless it was some time before the family made it their principal seat. Margaret, who retired to a nunnery on the death of her husband, left Barmston to her fourth son, Matthew, and Thomas, the heir, lived mainly at Roxby. However his son Matthew described himself as 'of Barmston' and it is an indication of their growing importance in the area that, upon the Dissolution of Monasteries by Henry VIII in 1539 and the transfer of all their property to the king, Matthew Boynton was appointed chief steward of all that in Yorkshire and Lincolnshire, a lucrative position.

The Boynton family, by a combination of judicious marriage and crown patronage, was now definitely on the up and was able to survive the potential disaster of the property going into wardship in the next generation. Thomas, son of Matthew, was under age when his father died and was married off to Jane Fairfax of Gilling. She died childless and Thomas then married Frances Frobisher of Doncaster, a cousin of the explorer, who provided the heir. His latest wife was Alice Tempest.

Thomas is of special interest because he is the first of the Boyntons to have a visible record in Burton Agnes Hall. Above the alabaster chimney-piece depicting the wise and foolish virgins in the Great Hall is another, thought to have been brought from Barmston Hall, of carved wood bearing the arms of Sir Thomas Boynton and his three wives which appears to have been encased in a classical entablature by Sir Griffith Boynton, the sixth baronet whose own achievement and motto surmount it. Thomas is also important because in his person the Boyntons now officially enter the government of county and country. In 1576 he was High Sheriff of Yorkshire and in 1571 became MP for Boroughbridge. He was also considered one of the four most fit men eligible for a vacancy on the Council of the North when he was described as being 'rich in lands and possessions', but in the event not appointed.

However in 1602 his son Francis did become a member, joining his near neighbour Sir Henry Griffith, and like him he appears to have celebrated the occasion by building, for the manor house at Barmston dates from about this time. In 1603 when James VI was on his way south, Francis attended him in York where he received his knighthood. Francis was a man of strong religious beliefs and would probably have described himnself as a Calvinist, greatly opposed to the practices of catholicism. In his will he directed that there should be no extravagance at his funeral. It is not unreasonable to assume that Sir Henry and Sir Francis found each other congenial and that the eventual marriage of their children Frances and Matthew, besides being an excellent potential property transaction, gave genuine pleasure to both families.

Matthew Boynton: First Baronet and Founder of the Boyntons of Burton Agnes 1591 - 1647

Though Matthew Boynton himself never owned Burton Agnes Hall, as father of the eventual heir by his marriage to Frances Griffith, as the first baronet, and because his life is so interesting and is interwoven with so many local and national events of the highly disturbed and disturbing times in which he lived, his story is well worth telling.

The third child, but the first to survive infancy, of Sir Francis Boynton and his wife Dorothy Place, he was baptised at Barmston on 26th January 1591, and was followed by a sister, Dorothy. Like the Griffiths, though several babies were born to them the Boyntons ended up with just one son and one daughter, unhappily quite usual for their time.

On 9th April 1618 Matthew was in London and was knighted at the medieval Palace of Whitehall. The following year he became a baronet. The introduction of this rank in 1611 for 200 of the top gentry was to raise money for the settlement of Ireland, the king thinking, rightly, that they would be happy to pay for the privilege of being raised above their gentlemen neighbours and pass that privilege down to their male heirs since, unlike the Knighthood, it was to be hereditary. They were still styled 'Sir', but the suffix Baronet, usually abbreviated to 'Bart.' or 'Bt.' was added after the surname. Matthew Boynton paid the going rate of £1,100 for his baronetcy, but it is thought that it was refunded later, why we do not know.

It did not take long for the idea of keeping it to just a few to be eroded; James I, a wild spendthrift where personal pleasures, like court masques and presents to favourites were concerned, and perpetually strapped for cash, proceeded to milk the scheme as hard as he could. While there were some gentlemen, Sir Henry Griffith being one, who were not persuaded of the value of the new honour, Matthew Boynton became the first of a line of 13 Boynton baronets, the title only dying out in the present century.

Matthew came into his Boynton inheritance on the death of his father in 1617 and married the following year. He soon entered public life becoming MP for Hedon from 1621-23. In the hierarchy of the House of Commons the best constituencies were the counties but as these were in the hands of their leading families, noble gentlemen were happy to sit as borough members, the boroughs thinking it added to their standing to have a member of the landed gentry as their MP rather than one of their own leading tradesmen.

The Parliament was called because the king needed it to vote him funds to pursue an active foreign policy. For peace-loving James, who also wanted to unite the protestants and catholics at home, times were very difficult. He looked likely to be drawn into a European war to support his daughter's husband, the new King of Bohemia, and he was also trying to cement his alliance with Spain by marrying his son Charles to the Spanish — catholic — Infanta. Parliament wanted war with Spain, firm measures against the catholics and Charles to marry a protestant. King and Parliament were thus deeply divided and James, very conscious of his position as king by divine right, threatened to punish those who failed to support him. The Commons responded by a Protestation asserting their rights; James went to the new Banqueting Hall in Whitehall, called for the Commons Journal where the Protestation was recorded, and in a dramatic gesture of royal displeasure and power, tore it out.

This eventful baptism into the government of the country undoubtedly had bearing on Matthew's future conduct when war between monarch and parliament became inevitable. Meanwhile he did his duty as a man of affairs. He was selected to collect the forced loan to pay for the Spanish War demanded in March 1626 by the new king, Charles I, and in 1628 reluctantly became High Sheriff of Yorkshire. He had been shortlisted four times before, asking on one occasion to be excused on account of his youth (he was 35!). Besides all the other duties already described Matthew had to collect the unpopular 'ship money' for Charles who, carrying on the war with parliament started by his father and unable to get it to vote him sufficient revenue, extended the tax normally paid by ports in lieu of the boats they used to provide for the navy to the whole of the country.

In the same year Sir John Hotham was asked for his opinion on Sir Matthew and his friend and neighbour Sir William Constable of Flamborough as possible Deputy Lieutenants of Yorkshire (i.e. responsible for its military preparedness) and wrote,

"I think without exception they are the ablest and best affected to do his majestie's service in respect of their undoubted affection to religion which in these parts is not easie to find in gentlemen of prime ranke."

Young Sir Henry Griffith was not considered to be as able.

In July 1634 Matthew's wife Frances died, aged 35, having born him 12 children. She was buried in the little church at Roxby, built by her husband's ancestor Sir William Boynton whose grave is in front of the altar, and close by her home high on the bleak Yorkshire Moors overlooking the North Sea. The flat table tomb supported by marble urns bears the following inscription,

"Here lyeth the bodie of the Lady Frances Boynton sometimes wife of Sr. Matthew Boynton of Barmston, Knight and Baronet, Daughter of Sr. Henry Griffith of Burton Agnes, Knt. A Familie descended from Ancient and Honorable Ancestors.

Her life much more remarkable for graces than for days Yet in that more than ordinarilye abbreviated tyme her exact and holy Pilgrimage, the effects whereof in her Prudent and Provident disposing of all things pertaining to the duty of her Sex. As also in the indefatigable dilligence in the faithfull Education of her children was conspicuously manifested, That beside the good acceptance thereof which God testified to her in a numerous Posteritie, Shee had also hereby ingroven soe deep an impression in the hearts of all that knew her pious conversation (that were it not that Mortalitie doth deface the memorie of things) Shee needed no other monument.

She dyed about ye 3d of July in ye yeare of her age 36 Anno Ani 1634.

The said Sir Matthew Boynton to manifest his love for so well deserving wife hath with his own hand inscribed and caused to be erected this marble."

It was surely a happy marriage and the loss of Frances must have been deeply felt by her grieving husband and ten surviving children, the youngest, Marmaduke and Gustavus, babies of two and one. (It would seem that the Boyntons, having used up the good old family names of Francis, Henry, Matthew, etc. were now well into flights of fancy).

It also confirms the view that, to their contemporaries, the Boynton household would certainly be thought of as Puritan. To begin with this was no handicap; Puritans were diligent and hard-working, paying attention to detail in all aspects of life, certainly not retiring from the world, nor, except in extreme cases denying themselves the fruits of their labours which, because of these qualities were often considerable, but avoiding show in dress and particularly disliking elaborate funerals. All this was perfectly acceptable to the authorities and indeed because of their honesty and conscientiousness they were often appointed to posts of responsibility as we have seen with Matthew Boynton. It was their manner of religious observance that began to bring problems.

At first their daily domestic round of prayers, Bible-reading and religious

Roxby church with (foreground) all that remains of what was probably the home of Frances and Matthew Boynton.

Frances Boynton's tomb in Roxby church.

instruction for the young caused no public offence, but by the time we are speaking of attitudes had polarised. Puritans were being persecuted as much as Catholics and their lifestyle was ridiculed. The death of Frances appears to have driven Matthew to taking reckless consolation in his religion, ignoring the probable consequences, for in the same year he was asked to explain his attendance at 'Conventicles' — secret, illegal prayer-meetings and, in a further act of defiance against the law, he gave refuge in his household to Henry Jessey, a clergyman who had been dismissed from his living by opposing what many thought of as pro-catholic practises introduced by Archbishop Laud. Jessey preached regularly at Barmston and Roxby.

By the following year his dislike of the way things were going and the threat of prosecution determined him to emigrate to New England. He decided to settle in southern Connecticut where Lord Saye and Sele, one of the leading anti-Laudians, had a grant of land. It was necessary to move cautiously as his departure could be prevented so, as a preliminary, in 1636 he moved his family, which now included his new wife Katherine, the widow of Robert Stapylton of York, to his London house in Highgate. He then sent members of his household out to find — build? — a house big enough for what he referred to as his large family (the term would include his servants as well as his numerous children). Correspondence survives between him and John Winthrop the younger about their welfare, directed through a friend as the official attitude to emigration was hardening still further and land was being forfeited to the government. Perhaps because of this Sir Matthew began to have doubts leading to the abandonment of all his plans, far advanced though they were. His servants could choose either to remain in Connecticut or return home.

But things continued to deteriorate. At the end of 1637 Matthew sold a small amount of land, settled the bulk of his estates on Puritan friends and relatives to act as trustees and the next year successfully made the move initially to Haarlem and then with his friend Sir William Constable to Arnhem where, with other English families who found refuge in Dutch towns at this time, they were able to practise their religion in peace.

An earlier historian wrote, "*he being a religious gentleman that gave much countenance and shelter to the puritans, and scrupling conformity to the injunctions imposed in those times was so troubled and prosecuted (*persecuted) *that he was forced.... to go to Holland.*"

It is thought that the portrait of Matthew, Katherine and three children which hangs in the Great Hall at Burton Agnes was painted while they were in Holland. There is a record of an inscription which was once attached to it,

"Nescio virtus stare loco
anno domino 1639
peregrinationis
sucudo"

The Latin is untranslatable but confirms that they were abroad in 1639 and we know that in 1640 Matthew and Katherine had a son whom they named Peregrine. Who the children are in the portrait is a puzzle. One source says Peregrine was the second child of the marriage, in which case the baby in the picture could be the elder one and the other two Frances's youngest, Marmaduke and Gustavus, the latter aged about seven and not yet breeched.

Both Katherine's children died young. Peregrine was buried in Barmston church under a monument identical to that of Frances in Roxby Church but it has since been dismantled and a copy of the inscription it once bore is now on a 19th century brass plate in the south aisle.

"In memorie of Peregrine Boynton sonne to Sir Matthew Boynton, Bart, and his Lady Katherine daughter of Viscount Fairfax of Gilling whom God gave unto them when they were strangers in a forraine land and endowed him with as much to endear him to his parents as his years could be capable of remarkable in many ways but for his love and observance of them beyond what is found in those of his yeares this sweet child finished his life ye 28 of August, Anno Dni 1645 being five years and five months old.
His mother in memorie of her sonne that was tenderly beloved in her eyes erected this marble."

After his first two years it is unlikely that the little boy saw much of his father in his short life, for Matthew immediately became heavily involved in the Civil War.

When the Royalist and Parliamentary parties began to form Matthew Boynton, like most other Puritans, was naturally drawn to the side of Parliament thus putting him against his late wife's brother, Henry Griffith. Matthew's is the first signature on *"The Petition of the Knights, Gentlemen, Freeholders and others, the Inhabitants of the County and City of York presented to the Honourable House of Commons now assembled in Parliament, wherein they humbly offer to billet and Mayntain at their own charge 300 of their horse and 3,000 of their Trained Bands within their own Shire for three Months, if the Parliament shall think fit."* He was fully prepared to fight and indeed, together with his second son, Colonel Matthew Boynton, saw active service throughout the war.

They appear to have spent much of their time locally, particularly in Hull and Scarborough and were in Beverley on one eventful occasion when the younger Boynton took prisoner Sir John Hotham, who despite his heroic stance on Hull battlements, had been assailed by terrible doubts about his position and eventually changed sides. Attempting to reach his house at Scorborough he was captured in Saturday Market Place by young Matthew who named him a traitor to the Commonwealth. Sir John's son Captain Hotham was also taken prisoner; they were kept in the Tower of London and the following January both were beheaded. Besides being good friends in the past the Boyntons were relatives of Sir John's present wife, a further example of the dreadful personal stress the war subjected people to.

1644 saw Sir Matthew in charge of the Hull garrison, and at the beginning of 1645 he took over the forces surrounding Scarborough Castle — that unhappy stronghold changing hands seven times in seven years. It was commanded by Hugh Cholmley, a son of Matthew's neighbour at Roxby, Sir Richard Cholmley, who had started the war a strong Parliamentarian having been personally threatened by Charles I — "You, Sir Hugh, shall hang", but changed sides when he felt the Parliamentarians had gone too far. The siege, which lasted twelve months, was over on 18th February 1645 by which time everything which could possibly be eaten inside the castle had been consumed. Matthew wrote, "*They surrendered with honour, and the inmates marched out or were carried out like a procession of spectres with Sir Hugh at the point of starvation.*"

Matthew, by then aged 54, was no doubt glad to hand over the governorship of the castle to his son. Captain Boynton was described at the time as "*of a local family that had given unstinted service throughout the war, father just appointed one of Scarborough's new MPs.*"

Sir Matthew had two more years' left, two years which, although they saw the execution of Archbishop Laud and Charles I a prisoner in the hands of Parliament, were also marred for him by deep divisions amongst the Parliamentarians and it is possible that he suffered arrest by the army. Loving husband, family man, deeply committed to his religion, despite his opposition to the king there must have been something about his formidable rectitude that kept him in public office. He was a JP throughout all the troubles. Constable and Hotham were removed from the bench and others on their side were threatened with punishment but he survived to die in his bed at Highgate in 1649.

He was buried in St. Andrew's church Holborn. In 1645 the living of the minister, the Rev. John Hackett was sequestered by Parliament because he continued to use the Book of Common Prayer, which attracted attention because many notable Parliamentarians lived in the parish. He was replaced by a succession of eminent Puritans which must account for Matthew's choice of his final resting place. There is no trace of it now. The church was rebuilt by Sir Christopher Wren in 1686 and largely rebuilt a second time after being bombed in 1942.

At Burton Agnes Hall the Civil War is recalled by two portraits, one a copy of the famous painting of Oliver Cromwell by Robert Walker, and a small painting of Captain Matthew Boynton in armour.

CHAPTER SEVEN
BURTON AGNES HALL COMES TO THE BOYNTONS

Sir Francis Boynton, 2nd Baronet 1618 - 1695

Francis Boynton was born at Roxby on 31st August 1618, the second child and heir of Sir Matthew Boynton of Barmston and his wife Frances, née Griffith. Their first baby, Henry, was born and died the previous year.

He was sent to board at school in Beverley, probably from the age of nine to eighteen when he went to Emmanuel College, Cambridge. The rather misleadingly titled Free School at Beverley — pupils paid, it had been freed from church control at the Reformation — was like all other schools in the country, a boys' grammar school, that is to say where Latin and Greek were principally taught, but also arithmetic and the rudiments of some other subjects. Tradition gives the date 703 as the year of its foundation but it would be safer to say it was set up sometime in the early middle ages in order to train choristers, clerks and priests for what was to become the great collegiate church of Beverley Minster. It now existed not only to prepare boys for the church but also the professions or just to give what was considered at the time a good education. Until the middle of the 18th century the reputation of all schools depended on the Master and boys were sent to the nearest good one. The Master in Francis Boynton's time was John Pomeroy, described as 'learned and skilful' and who sent many boys to Cambridge. He thus attracted the patronage of the leading county families such as the Boyntons the Wartons and the Hildyards but Francis's schoolfellows also included the sons of a clothshearer and a butcher.

He married, probably in 1637, Constance, a daughter of the Lord Saye and Sele from whom his father had purchased land in Connecticut and one of the leading Parliamentarians throughout the Civil War. He did not therefore accompany his father and the rest of the family into exile in Holland but remained with his bride at her father's house, Broughton Castle in Oxfordshire, famous for its 'room that hath no ears', jutting out over the moat where the Parliamentarians could make their plans without fear of being overheard. Since a marriage was arranged between their children Sir Matthew and Lord Saye and Sele must have been on close terms and this gives rise to the supposition that Matthew must have been one of those plotters from time to time.

This marriage into the nobility marks the apogee of the Boyntons social advancement and indeed, with the acquisition of the Griffith property, they are now also at the height of their wealth. The couple had a house in Hull where at least two of their seven children were born, so Francis may have had some commercial interests. Other than that, though he styled himself as 'of Burton Agnes' in 1654 when he inherited it, he lived mostly at Barmston 'in great hospitality' according to a contemporary account. This is rather an old-fashioned phrase for the time indicating that Sir Francis kept open house for all comers in the style of the previous century and, looking at his expansive figure in his picture at Burton Agnes, one can easily see him as the genial host presiding at a well laden board. Constance too, in the companion painting, seems to have put on a lot of weight since she sat for the grand romantic portrait of her as a young bride. Francis died 'of a fever' at the relatively advanced age of 76, outliving his heir William (named with due deference to rank after his grandather Saye and Sele) so all that hospitality cannot have done him much harm.

This was the age of the final consolidation of estates. A great reshuffling of land went on as owners sold distant manors and bought those that adjoined their main property. In this way Francis, with the consent of his heir William, broke the final links with his mother's ancestral home in Staffordshire and sold Wychnor with its remaining acres for £9,000, at the same time buying up any suitable plots to round off his Yorkshire estate.

In the aftermath of all the Civil War problems there was much concern to establish watertight legal rights to estates for future generations. Known as 'strict settlements' they went into considerable detail as to the different uses of various parts of the property, who was to live in which house, how it was to be inherited by descendants yet unborn so that it was virtually impossible to split it up, then an owner's worst nightmare. The strict settlement Francis made upon William's marriage in 1661 is the first in East Yorkshire and was immediately followed by all the other landowners.

Though there is no portrait of William at Burton Agnes two other sons of Francis can be seen — Nathaniel, a handsome young man who died unmarried at the age of 28 as the result of a riding accident and Henry who, as was now usual with younger sons, entered the church becoming Rector of Barmston.

William Boynton goes to live at Burton Agnes

William Boynton, heir to his father Sir Francis, is important as the first of his family to make Burton Agnes his home. It is likely that the big house had been empty for some time, certainly since the death of young Sir Henry in 1654 and as he had made Wychnor his main residence, in his lifetime it was probably only used when he came up on business.

The events leading to William's occupancy are a fascinating illustration of the times. During his financial difficulties in the Civil War Henry Griffith had used the manor of Burton Agnes as collateral for a mortgage of £2,000 he had secured from Arthur Ingram of Knottingley. In 1653 he seems to have had further cash flow problems and he and his cousin Francis Boynton, by now his acknowledged heir and reconciled, jointly conveyed Burton Agnes for 99 years to the trustees of the late John Barnard who had been a Hull merchant and presumably known to Francis, receiving £4,000, part of which Henry used to clear the mortgage. Two days after the conveyance it was leased back to Sir Henry at a rent of £400 for 21 years and a peppercorn thereafter. Henry may have known he was mortally ill, he died the following year, and was putting his affairs in order.

In 1661 William married Elizabeth, John Barnard's daughter, and as part of the marriage settlement the lease of Burton Agnes was surrendered to him. Was this the outcome of a long-term business plan? The end of the story came after William's death when Elizabeth, back in legal possession of the house, sold it to her son Griffith for £10,000, possibly a nominal sum for the purpose of the conveyance document. All we can be certain is that Burton Agnes now legally belonged entirely to the Boyntons and despite some hairy moments in the future would remain so.

When William's sister Frances married at the end of 1667 she and her husband George Whichcoat also went to live there but after 2½ years she died giving birth to twin boys, one baby dying within days and the other surviving to join his little cousins Griffith, Mary and Constance for only two years.

The Boyntons seem to have entered Parliament every other generation and now it was William's turn, but how times had changed. When his grandfather was MP for Scarborough it was under Cromwell; now the monarchy had been restored and Charles II was on the throne. But there was still trouble with religion though now it was Parliament which insisted by passing the Test Act in 1673 that only members of the Church of England could hold civil or military office, thus excluding Catholics and non-conformist protestants from public life until it was repealed in 1829. William had gone through the whole procedure. On 22nd June 1673, in Lissett Church on the Boynton estate about half way between Barmston and Burton Agnes, he received the sacrament according to the Anglican rites, he declared against the Catholic belief in transsubstantiation (whereby the bread and wine of the communion service is thought to become actually rather than symbolically the body and blood of Christ) and took the oath of supremacy and allegiance. He then received a certificate of affirmation.

William was now free to continue his family's connection with the borough of Hedon and became its MP in 1680. Parliament's main concern was the Royal succession; though the father of many illegitimate children, Charles' queen, Catherine of Braganza, had failed to provide him with an heir and the next in line, his brother James, Duke of York, was a Catholic. So, in fact, was Charles. Though this was suspected it was only confirmed by him on his deathbed, but it is not surprising when one remembers that the boys were brought up in exile by their Catholic mother, Henrietta Maria. Charles managed to foil Parliament's attempts to pass the Exclusion Bill (to exclude James) and his brother succeeded peacefully in 1685. There was then a revolt by the Earl of Monmouth, son of Charles, whom many had wanted to be pronounced his heir, but it was overthrown and Monmouth was executed.

Fine full length court portraits of Charles II and James II are to be seen at Burton Agnes, but also one of Monmouth, a problem for anyone trying to work out the family's allegiances. Part of the answer is that the royal pair were introduced by Marcus Wickham-Boynton, the legacy of a friend. The significance of Monmouth is debatable.

The Warming Pan Baby Plot

In the house is a third painting which connects the Boynton family with the reign of James II. Just over 40 years ago we left Colonel Matthew Boynton holding Scarborough Castle for the Parliamentarians. By now the castle was roofless and though building supplies could have been brought in by sea none was forthcoming nor, despite constant requests, was any money provided for his troops' provision. Completely disillusioned, Colonel Boynton put a red flag on the castle wall and declared his allegiance to the imprisoned King and the Prince of Wales. At the end of six months, the last three of which he had been besieged, Matthew and his soldiers were allowed to surrender on astonishingly generous terms — they marched out 'drums beating, muskets laden, bandolier filled and bullet in mouth (to) lay down their arms' and return home free men.

But Matthew did not return home, he went to join the Prince of Wales and in 1651 he was with the army that the Prince, since the execution of his father styling himself Charles II, had collected in Scotland and, coming south, died at the Battle of Wigan Lane.

Matthew left two little girls who, when old enough, in acknowledgement of their father's change of heart, were taken into royal service and suitable marriages arranged for them. Both became Ladies-in-Waiting at the court of Charles II and later to Queen Mary of Modena second wife of James II. By now James had made himself most unpopular and his religion did nothing to help but his heir was his daughter Mary, married to Prince William of Orange, and as both were staunch protestants the country was mostly prepared for events to take their course until the Queen, after fifteen years of childless marriage, produced a baby son. Consternation reigned as the baby now became heir and word was put about that it was a papist plot, the infant was not the Queen's but had been introduced into her bed in a warming-pan.

Isabella and Katherine, who had both been present at the birth, gave evidence at the subsequent Inquiry, but it was discounted on the grounds that they were catholics, (their grandparents would have been horrified), party to the plot and unlikely to say anything to hurt the 'pretend' prince and his parents.

The painting, of no artistic merit but of great interest as a piece of propaganda, shows the king and queen under a canopy and the baby in the centre with a wet-nurse surrounded by attendants while in the forefront are various allegorical figures.

Shortly afterwards Prince William landed at the head of an army and the king was invited to abdicate and join his family in exile in France. William and Mary ascended the throne as joint monarchs. The disputed baby grew up to be known as the Old Pretender and his son the Young Pretender or, more romantically, Bonnie Prince Charlie.

Katherine's husband was Richard, Earl of Tyrconnell, rabid catholic and described as 'terrifying and anti-English'. He was made lord Lieutenant of Ireland and held the country for James after he fled to France. Subsequently James went to Ireland but he and Tyrconnell were defeated by William at the Battle of the Boyne, Charles Carter, Isabella's second husband (her first was Lord Rosscommon) being one of William's supporters.

William Boynton died in 1689, six years before his father, so never came into his inheritance. His widow Elizabeth lived on for many years doing much charitable work in the village and in her will left money for the building of a hospital for the widows of four tenants. Eventually she went to live with her daughter Constance who had married Richard Kirshaw the Rector of Ripley, where she died. A portrait of Constance Kirshaw hangs at Burton Agnes.

CHAPTER EIGHT
THE HOUSE IN THE 18th CENTURY

Sir Griffith Boynton, 3rd Baronet 1665 - 1730

To preserve the Griffith name, of which he was very proud, William Boynton gave it to his eldest (and only) son as a Christian name and thereby initiated a family tradition. At the age of about 12 young Griffith was painted by John Riley, one of the foremost portraitists of the time, the picture now hanging in the Small Hall. He went up to University, considered a suitable finishing school for young Gentlemen, and graduated from Clare College, Cambridge in 1682. However neither he nor any succeeding Boynton appears to have gone on that further education trip usually thought so necessary by the upper classes, the Grand Tour, and so there are no souvenirs in the shape of classical statuary or paintings by Canaletto in Burton Agnes Hall.

Old Sir Francis finally died in 1695 and Griffith, aged thirty and so far unmarried, became the third Baronet and owner of Burton Agnes Hall, Barmston Hall and the rest of the estate.

He decided to make Burton Agnes, where he had been born and brought up, his country seat, as he would have put it, though of course he must also have a London house and acquired one in Pall Mall. But what to do about the house at Burton Agnes? In the 90 or so years since it was first inhabited lifestyles and architecture had changed completely; Sir Henry Griffith's house and all those others like it were constructed around the Great Hall, which meant every manor house in the country built before about 1650, was totally out of date.

Architecture finally acknowledged what had been fact for hundreds of years that, except at times of special festivity, master and servants no longer ate together in the Hall, neither were the servants the younger sons of the lord of the manor's equals but a different and lower class altogether and the less seen the better. In the fashionable new houses the Great Hall had given way to the Entrance Hall with the stairs sweeping up to the grand entertaining rooms on the first floor. Servants had a separate hall provided for their needs, usually near the kitchen, and both these rooms were quite often put in the basement from where another new idea, a maze of back stairs, serviced the apartments of the owner, his family and guests, leading eventually to the servants' bedrooms in the attic. Personal attendants still slept within earshot in a small room off that of their master or mistress whose close stool was often kept in the same room; now, of course, these could be emptied via the back stairs which their owners thought a great improvement. Many servants were now women. Life had become much daintier, houses were kept cleaner, people liked to collect porcelain ornaments and other bric-a-brac which needed careful dusting: women were better at these things.

Houses looked different too. During the upheavals of the middle of the century many people had taken refuge on the continent, young men toured it, and Dutch King William brought its ideas and practitioners with him. Not surprisingly continental styles of architecture originating in Italy and developed by Palladio from the classical buildings of ancient civilisations became popular. Windows changed shape; gone were the stone mullions and transoms and they became taller and narrower and uniformly arranged on the facade. Improvements in glass-making gave larger panes which were held by wooden glazing bars instead of lead and they now opened up and down by means of sash cords rather than outwards on side hinges.

If you were *nouveau riche* and putting together a new estate you could build your house from scratch to the new designs. Old Money, if there was plenty of it, could redesign the whole of a house as at Chatsworth, but most owners, like Griffith Boynton, decided what were necessary modernisations, did those and left the rest; what was most necessary was that which was seen by his visitors. The first alterations at Burton Agnes are now described as if they were all part of the same scheme and all undertaken by Sir Griffith Boynton; this may not have been the case, but in the absence of documentary evidence we can only go on style and supposition.

No rooms were added and nothing demolished; from the outside the only noticeable difference is in the windows where those flat ones to the principal rooms were changed to the new design. All the rest retained their original shape and size and their leaded glazing bars, these finally being replaced by wood in the 19th century.

It would have been possible to have put a new staircase and gallery in the Great Hall which would have given much better access to the bedrooms but the Screen would have had to go and the expense would have been enormous. Instead the 'lord's end' was provided with three arched openings, one giving on to the stairs, the bottom flight of which was swung round 90 degrees, one opening into the Small Hall and one, for symmetry, framing the end window. These were flanked by the 17th century carvings of classical gods and goddesses which may previously have ranged along the wall behind the High Table, Sol properly in the middle as indicated by the shape of his pedestal. The room was also given a new ceiling in high relief featuring a Greek Key design with beautifully turned corners, obviously the work of master craftsmen. Unfortunately the central circular design from the middle of which hangs the lantern throws the room off balance. The fireplace is correctly positioned in the centre of its wall, calculating from the wall of the Screens Passage. The ceiling has to use the Screen as the end wall, therefore its centre motif and the fireplace do not align. The Great Hall modernisation was completed by covering he wooden floor with black and white tiles.

Sir Griffith was one ahead of most of his contemporaries — he already had back stairs, though when they were built they were more secondary than back and led from the screens passage to the subsidiary family bedrooms, the only other access being through the master bedroom off the upstairs Withdrawing Room. However they could be turned to rise from the service area passage and the original opening to them together with two of the three medieval style archways in the long wall of the Screens Passage was blocked off.

Since it was now inappropriate for the family to use these stairs access to the bedrooms was made by building a narrow two storey extension along the south wall of the courtyard, the upper forming a passage with a new doorway off the main stairs. A corresponding single-storey corridor was built along the north side of the courtyard giving weatherproof access to the chapel (which may well have found another use by now) and the north east corner of the house.

If houses were getting cleaner so were people which meant more work for the wash-house which was rather inconveniently placed immediately below Sir Griffith's quarters with a far from soundproof ceiling. The solution was to convert the old manor house, now shrunk back to Roger de Stutevilles's original building, into a new modern laundry and probably at the same time its south and east walls were given their brick casing and sash windows to match its big neighbour.

At his end of the Great Hall Sir Griffith did away with the Painted Room and created the area known today as the Garden Gallery which has access to the formal pleasure grounds, and, through arches which he inserted, to the staircase.

He now undertook a major work of interior redecoration — he stripped the carved oak panelling from three rooms and replaced it with the new painted pine bolection panelling. The Garden Gallery was one, the Withdrawing Room next to it and the great High Dining Room the other two. What must have been lost, particularly in the Dining Room, which had been Sir Henry's Great Chamber and the best room in the house, hardly bears thinking about.

The former 'Painted Room', now the Garden Gallery,
showing panelling and arches introduced by the 3rd Baronet
and also some of the modern paintings collected by Marcus Wickham-Boynton.

Looking at it from Griffith's point of view he was no doubt glad to be rid of the gloomy old stuff with its designs picked out in the heavy gilding and primary blues and reds beloved of the Tudors and Stuarts and bring some light and delicate colour into the rooms. One has to remember that, when first applied to the walls, the oak panelling would have been the pale honey colour of newly-sawn wood. All untreated panelling of the time shows what natural aging, open fires and the smoke from tallow candles can do.

The Withdrawing Room door into the Garden Gallery was moved from the left to the right side of the fireplace, aligning it with the door from the downstairs dining room. This was very much in accordance with contemporary planning. In new houses the ideal was to line up the doors to a series of rooms so precisely that, peering through the keyhole of the first, one could see the light from a candle shining through the keyhole of the last, though one wonders how often this was achieved. The room was completed with overdoor paintings of Queen Anne and her husband Prince George of Denmark, thus dating this particular work to somewhere between 1702 and 1714.

The Low Dining Room was promoted to the main and only one. Long gone were the stately processions of the lord's food through the respectful household in the Great Hall and up the stairs. Eating was much less formal and the advantage of having the dining room somewhat nearer the kitchen was acknowledged. Now on a fine day the company could progress through the Withdrawing Room (now just 'Drawing Room') to the garden, a delightful arrangement. Why wasn't the panelling replaced in the Dining Room (the present Red Drawing Room)? One theory is that instead it was covered with fabric hangings fixed to battens. Whatever the reason we are thankful for it today. The room was given a new ceiling, however, again featuring the Greek Key design though more restrained than that in the great Hall.

The old High Dining Room with its new panelling was now furnished as a sitting room and became that height of fashion, a delightful 'salon', usually anglicised to Saloon. Its door off the staircase was given a suitably classical architrave and where there had probably been a door to the State Guest Apartment lobby a large opening was made with a similar surround. In the apartment itself the ante-room between the two bedrooms was shortened by providing a passage way to the Queen's Room with some alteration to the door that necessitated the removal of the internal porch, and of St. Barbara to the closet door.

Towards the end of Sir Griffith's life it became the rage to build houses with classical facades and incorporate 'Palladian' windows. He forebore to stick a pediment on the front of Burton Agnes Hall but he did furnish each end of the Long Gallery with a huge window in the new style.

Sir Griffith is remembered for two other works; be built a hospital at Barmston 'for decayed servants of his family' and in Burton Agnes church he installed seating in the nave and aisles that is still there and constructed a family pew under an imposing arch very similar to those in the Great Hall of his house.

In 1712, when he was 38, Sir Griffith Boynton found time to think of other things, perhaps the succession, and brought a bride to Burton Agnes. The lady was Adriana Sykes, daughter of John Sykes, a merchant of Dort, Holland but

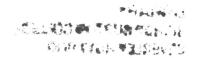

sadly she was not very robust and died, childless, 'after a lingering illness' at their London house in Pall Mall, in December 1724. He was married again in 1728, to Rebecca White, but died himself, still without children, two years later at his new London house in Great Ormonde Street, then just being developed. He left to his wife his coach and any two horses of his six with harness, also the furniture at Great Ormonde Street, together with all his personal belongings that were in the house and three cabinets, two of which appear to be now at Burton Agnes, one inlaid with stone figures of birds which is in the Great Hall and a larger black one with painted scenes inside the doors and opening top, now in the Queen's Room. There are portraits of each of Sir Griffith's wives and two of him at Burton Agnes. Rebecca lived only a further two years and was buried at Burton Agnes on 23rd October 1732.

So no direct heir but a lot to remind us of the third Baronet in Burton Agnes Hall and while one would love to be able to see the old house perfectly preserved as it was built that would deny both the existence of the family that kept it going and the opportunity to see in Sir Griffith's alterations such an accurate depiction of the taste of his time.

Sir Francis Boynton, 4th Baronet 1672 - 1739

The Rev. Henry Boynton, Rector of Barmston, uncle to Sir Griffith also lived at Burton Agnes and his children were born and brought up there. Though his eldest son Francis was in line to succeed his cousin to the baronetcy, while Griffith was alive he must be presumed to provide himself with an heir. Thus Francis was brought up to earn his own living. Like his grandfather he went to Beverley Free School, at that time under one of its most famous heads, the Rev. Joseph Lambert who, having been appointed at the early age of 24, remained for 42 years and was the first of a series of masters who, in the late 17th and 18th century, put Beverley in the front rank of northern schools. Celia Fiennes wrote in 1697, the year after Francis left to go up to Cambridge,

> "(in Beverley) *There is a very good free schoole for boys, they say the best in England for learning and care, which makes it filled with Gentlemens Sons beside the free Schollars from all parts.*"

The free scholars were there courtesy of the many legacies with which Beverley people had shown their appreciation of the school. In addition, from the early 16th century, there had been two scholarship funds to enable boys to go to St. John's College Cambridge, and, because of the connection, in fact the majority of boys going on to higher education went to St. John's including Francis. We know Francis's second son also went to Beverley and there may well have been other Boyntons — there is a suggestion that Matthew, the first baronet, was a pupil there (his adversary at Scarborough, Sir Hugh Cholmley, certainly was) but present research limits us to the names of those boys who went on to Cambridge at this time. After various vicissitudes in its long history the school evolved into the present Beverley Grammar School.

Francis went on to become a barrister-at-law of Gray's Inn and, in 1732 on the death of Sir Charles Hotham, Recorder of Beverley. This is an ancient office, the earliest occupants keeping a record of the courts and customs of a

LIBRARY
BISHOP BURTON COLLEGE
BEVERLEY HU17 8QG

town but by this time the Recorder acted as a local judge. He lived at what is now 15 North Bar Within (Carmichael's shop) nearly opposite St. Mary's Church where all the children of his marriage to Frances, daughter of James Hebblethwayte of Norton, were baptised and three of them buried, including William in infancy and Dorothy at the age of 14.

His wife, too, lies there, dying after a short illness in 1720. Francis was therefore a widower when he came to Burton Agnes Hall at the age of 52 and his daughter Constance, who, though only 16 at the time, had taken over the management of his household on the death of her mother, became its mistress. She remained unmarried until two years after her father died in 1739 having left her £100 in his will 'for the extraordinary care she had taken in directing his household affairs'. She was then 37, but in fact all Sir Francis' children married late, Griffith aged 33 and Francis 45 and had only two children between them. Adriana stayed single and lived to be 80.

Sir Francis remained Recorder of Beverley until his death in 1739 and was MP for Hedon from 1734. His portrait shows a man of open, good-humoured countenance, just the sort of person to merit this eulogy which is appended to the entry of his death in the Burton Agnes parish register,

> *"He was an affectionate husband, a tender parent, a kind master and amiable neighbour. The easiness and frankness of his temper led many into his acquaintance, and the more he was known the more he was esteemed. He judged a general civility a debt to mankind, was a stranger to those little arts which a great soul despises, and a good one detests, he was cheerful without levity and virtuous without frugality, he lived the life and died the death of the righteous."*

It is very possible that Sir Francis was responsible for some of the alterations attributed here to his cousin, he was rich enough for his wife had been the heiress of her grandfather, Sir William Cobb of Ottringham, and was a wealthy woman in her own right. Though the estate was in trust for his son Griffith, Sir Francis would have had the income. There are also references to floor levels being changed in 1730 and a mezzanine inserted in the Great Hall, but there is no evidence for this in the house. Certainly the old oak floor boards, no doubt dangerously worn by now and, like the panelling very dark, were replaced round about this time by pine with typical 'billiard cue' joins which can be seen in the upstairs Drawing Room. It also looks as though the joists had sagged somewhat towards the centre of the house and to level up the floors it was necessary to make a step to the State Guest Apartment entrance lobby.

Sir Griffith Boynton, 5th Baronet 1712 - 1761

This Griffith was born and named, while his father's cousin, the third baronet, was still — just — unmarried so perhaps there was already a thought that he might succeed. In May 1730 he followed his father to Gray's Inn, then also a fashionable place to spend a few terms at even for those who had no necessity to earn a living as a lawyer. Indeed by the Christmas his uncle had died, he knew where his future lay and at the age of 27 Burton Agnes Hall and the Boynton estates became his.

It was six years before he himself married, at St. George's Church Hanover Square London, Anne, the daughter of Thomas White of Tuxford, Nottinghamshire, who was MP for Retford. She was a year older than Griffith and in an age when it was a young woman's duty to secure a suitable husband for herself as soon as possible she must have felt relieved. There is a portrait of her, rather prim-faced, next to one of her husband in the Screens Passage at Burton Agnes; she appears to be wearing her wedding dress. If Sir Griffith was looking for an heir he would have been delighted that his bride became pregnant almost immediately, but in those days even more than now she was rather old for a first baby and in fact it killed her. A little boy was born on Saturday evening 22nd February 1743 at Wallingwells, Nottingham, and a few hours later his mother died. Lady Boynton was brought on her sad last journey home to Burton Agnes where she was buried the following Thursday. She had been married for nine months and 15 days.

Marriage, then the only appropriate career for young gentlewomen, was unfortunately also a hazardous one, many dying in childbirth. For the poor that usually meant the death of the baby too but the rich could hire a wet nurse and the infant Griffith remained in Wallingwells with his, surviving his bad start in life. His father did not remarry and one feels that Burton Agnes Hall cannot have been a very jolly place at this time; Sir Griffith's memorial in the church describes a modest man who 'chose to fill a private station with virtues that would have adorn'd a public one'.

Nevertheless, when appointed High Sheriff of Yorkshire in 1751, he put on the requisite show which cost him £437 3s. 9d. and includes such interesting items as a new wig for himself, six pairs of shoes for the trumpeters he had to provide for each of the three assizes, ale and beer for the judges and coal for their lodgings. When he went to attend the judges he was accompanied by 193 liverymen donated in numbers from 1 to 6 by all the nobles and gentry of the county and 16 halberdmen whose shaving he also had to pay for. Quite a performance.

In the middle of the 18th century the whole of Europe became seized with a passion for everything Chinese. In Austria Empress Maria Theresa spent a fortune importing Chinese wallpaper for the Blue Salon at Schonbrunn Palace while in England an article published in *The World* in 1753 proclaimed,

"According to the present prevailing whim, everything is Chinese, or in the Chinese taste: or, as it is sometimes more modestly expressed, 'partly after the Chinese Manner'. Chairs, tables, chimney-pieces, frames for looking glasses, and even our most vulgar utensils, are all reduced to this new-fangled standard; and without doors so universally has it spread, that every gate to a cow yard is in T's and Z's, and every hovel for the cows has bells hanging at the corners."

The writer may have been guilty of slight exaggeration, but certainly every one who could tried to have something of oriental appearance in his home and if you were rich enough you could have a whole Chinese Room which is what Sir Griffith converted the Drawing Room to. He obtained a large 12-section Coromandel screen (so called because they were imported from China via the

Coromandel coast of India), which on one side had a picture of a palace with several courtyards, showing incidentally that at this period the Chinese artists did not yet use perspective, and on the other a scene of trees, flowers, and birds, had it dismantled and applied the panels to the walls of the room. No one wall was long enough to accommodate the whole screen but by splitting it up and using some extra border almost the whole room could be covered, making Queen Anne and her husband, keeping an eye on things from above their respective doors, look somewhat out of place.

Above the Chinese Room fireplace is a very fine portrait of Sir Griffith by Philippe Mercier. Born in Berlin of French parents and much influenced by Watteau he set up a studio in York round about 1740 and painted many of the local gentry. Earlier he had been principal painter to Frederick, Prince of Wales, eldest son of George II, and in the National Portrait Gallery is a lovely picture of the prince and his sisters playing musical instruments entitled 'The Music Party'. At Burton Agnes is another charming Mercier called 'The Fishing Party'.

Sir Griffith Boynton, 5th Baronet, died in October 1761 at the relatively early age of 50 and was succeeded by his only child, his eighteen year old son.

Sir Griffith Boynton, 6th Baronet 1743 — 1778

Orphaned, and very eligible, the young baronet lost no time in finding a wife marrying, in York Minster the following May, Charlotte Topham, daughter of Francis Topham, a lawyer of Minster Yard. At 21 she was two years older than her husband. Their lives slipped easily into the usual pattern of the time, spending the summer and autumn at their country seat and the winter 'season' at their London house. Griffith enjoyed the delights of life in the capital and prolonged their stays as long as possible but Charlotte was homesick for her Yorkshire home.

By a stroke of good fortune this delightful letter from Charlotte to her housekeeper at Burton Agnes is preserved.

St. James's Place April 30th 1765
You will be much pleased to find by Sir Griffith's letter that our time is fixed for coming to Burton it gives me as much pleasure as it does you. I shall count the days with great impatience till we set out. Our people will set out in the Waggon next Monday and will be in York on the Monday following about twelve o'Clock. I would have them wait in York that day and set out for Burton on Tuesday morning so you must let the Horse come for them Early on Monday. We would not have our Waggon come, till we get to York so every thing will stay at Dr. Topham's till we write to have 'em removed which we shall not think of till we get to York. We would have our Bed Well air'd and then laid in two or three nights and the House Cleaned but none of the China taken out nor anything of that kind till we come home. The Ship which we sent our things in is not gon yet but will sail in a few days we hope you'll receive them safe, when you pay for their coming etc. with other that you paid incident to our London expenses I would not have you enter in your Books for I shall keep all our Bills that we have payed in London etc. together.
C. Boynton

Continued on page 81

The Norman Manor House built about 1174: north elevation showing the bricked up 1st floor entrance and ground floor arches cut to gain access to additional rooms since demolished.

The well dug for the Norman Manor House and the donkey wheel constructed at the beginning of the 17th century. The well remained the main water supply for Burton Agnes Hall until the 19th century.

The Norman Manor House: the first-floor Hall, re-windowed, heightened, and re-roofed mid 15th century.

The Norman Manor House: south and east elevations refaced in brick with sash windows to match the later house.

The Gatehouse with the coat of arms of James I.

Burton Agnes Hall: the west elevation showing alterations to 1st and second floor windows. Those on the ground floor to the former kitchen, buttery and plate house retain their original stone mullions and transoms. The Palladian window is at the west end of the Long Gallery.

The front door decorated with classical columns and the coats of arms of the Griffiths and Elizabeth I.

Detail of screen showing Reuben, Simeon and Levi, the first three sons of Jacob.
Photographs by Roland Wheeler-Osman, University of Hull Photographic & Copy Service.

The Great Hall screen.

St. Matthew: plasterwork, Great Hall screen.

Wise and Foolish Virgins: alabaster, above Great Hall fireplace.

Faith, Ho(o)pe and Charity; oak, Dining Room fireplace, originally in Long Gallery.
Photographs by Roland Wheeler-Osman, University of Hull Photographic & Copy Service.

Sir Matthew Boynton, 1st Baronet, his second wife Katherine and his three youngest children.

Sir Francis Boynton, 2nd Baronet.   *Sir Francis Boynton, 4th Baronet.*

Photographs by Roland Wheeler-Osman, University of Hull Photographic & Copy Service.

The downstairs Drawing Room, originally the Low Dining Room.

The Chinese Room, originally the Withdrawing Room.
Photograph by Roland Wheeler-Osman, University of Hull Photographic & Copy Service.

The Dining Room, originally the Still Room.

The upstairs Drawing Room. Originally Sir Henry Griffith's Great Chamber, then the third Baronet's 'salon', it was called the Ballroom in the Victorian era.

Sir Griffith Boynton, 5th Baronet.
Photograph by Roland Wheeler-Osman, University of Hull Photographic & Copy Service.

Sir Griffith Boynton, 6th Baronet.

Mary Hebblethwaite, wife of the 6th Baronet. Photographs by Roland Wheeler-Osman, University of Hull Photographic & Copy Service.

Sir Griffith Boynton, 7th Baronet.   *Sir Francis Boynton, 8th Baronet as a child.*

Sally Bucktrout, wife of the 8th Baronet.
Photographs by Roland Wheeler-Osman, University of Hull Photographic & Copy Service.

Mars and Venus in the Great Hall. *Terms in the King's Room frieze.*

Patience, Truth, Constancy and Victory above the Queen's Room fireplace. Patience holds a yoke, more commonly associated with Obedience. Truth (naked) has the sun; Constancy leans against a pillar and has her left hand in a brazier and Victory, holding a laurel wreath and palm, stands on a dragon symbolising the devil. On top of the columns are a phoenix, a pelican and an eagle. Photographs by Roland Wheeler-Osman, University of Hull Photographic & Copy Service.

Burton Agnes Hall: the restored Long Gallery.

View from the Long Gallery showing the Walled Garden.

Burton Agnes Hall, east elevation painted by William Marlow for the 6th Baronet showing the garden levelled and cleared of all planting, walks, etc. the retaining wall acting as a ha-ha. Photograph by Roland Wheeler-Osman, University of Hull Photographic & Copy Service.

View from the house showing the pond created by Marcus Wickham-Boynton and the prospect over the ha-ha. To the left of centre can be seen the 8th Baronet's cock pit.

Simon Cunliffe-Lister and Marcus Wickham-Boynton summer 1989.

Susan Cunliffe-Lister in the 'Jungle Garden'.

Giant Chess in the garden.

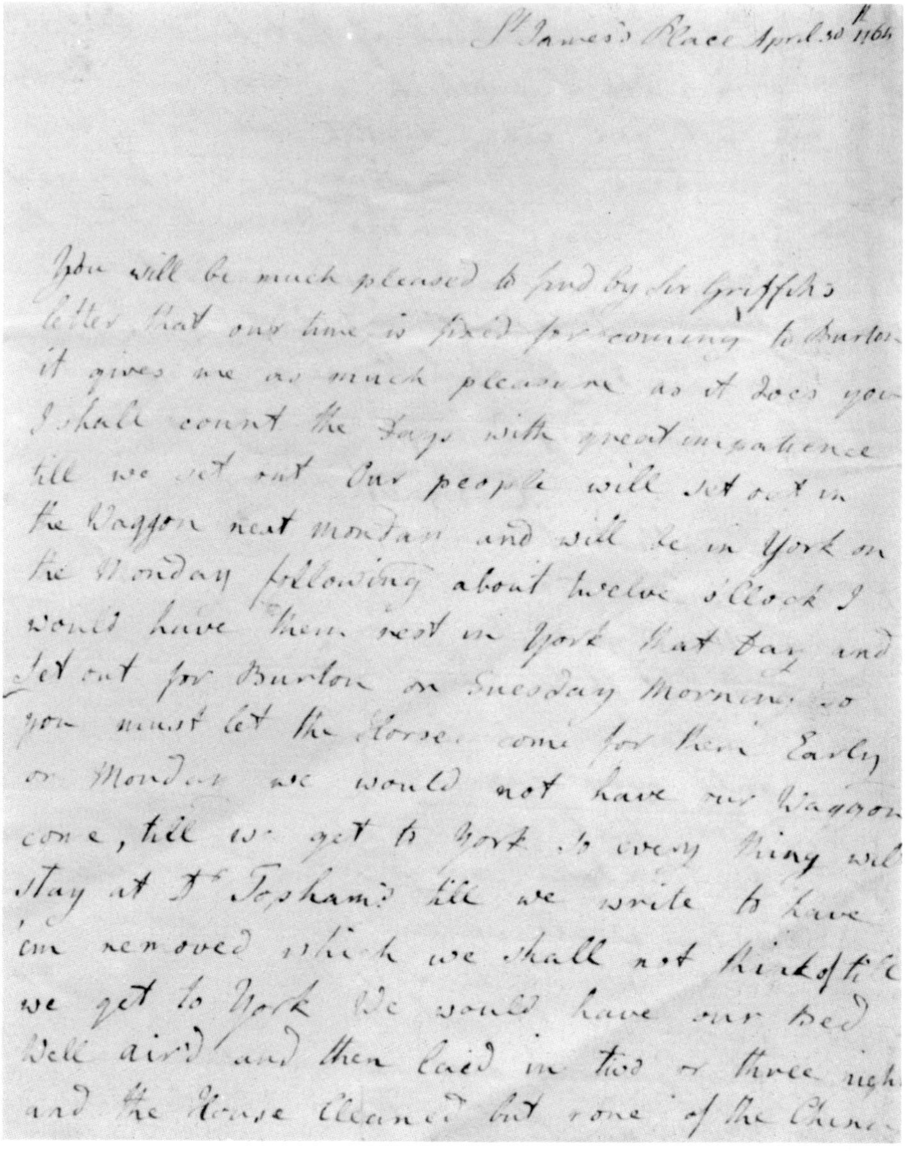

St James's Place April 30th 1764

[handwritten letter, partially legible]

You will be much pleased to find by Sir Griffith's
letter that our time is fixed for coming to Burton
it gives me as much pleasure as it does you
I shall count the days with great impatience
till we set out Our people will set out in
the Waggon next monday and will be in York on
the Monday following about twelve o'Clock I
would have them rest in York that day and
set out for Burton on Tuesday Morning so
you must let the Horses come for them Early
on Monday we would not have our Waggon
come, till we get to York so every thing will
stay at Dr Teshams till we write to have
em removed which we shall not think of till
we get to York We would have our bed
well air'd and then laid in two or three nights
and the House Cleaned but none of the Chin—

*Charlotte Boynton's letter with arrangements for their return from London
including (bottom) those for the airing of the bed.*

The Boyntons have a great deal of luggage to bring back from London, some their personal effects but also there is furniture and other items for the house purchased from the best places. The bulky items travel by water, probably to Bridlington, as the likelihood of damage in transit is much less than using the potholed roads. The arrangements for their bed are very interesting — who in the household risked getting a chill warming it up for its owners?

Charlotte had also spent some time planning little alterations that would make life more convenient and adds a postscript,

> *If Perrot is able to alter the door going into our Bedroom from the back stairs and that of Sir G I would have 'em set about 'em. They should open opposite to that door that goes into my dressing room and from the bed, they would be very little work, for in the Bedroom there would only be to fill the present door up and open another at the other side of the Bed which would be very easily done as the door and everything would be ready to put in. And that of Sir G's the door would be to take out and the pannel that came out of the other place would fill it up and then the door would go where the pannel came out of and for the passage there would only want a little new paper which you might get at Burlington (Bridlington) and Perrot would put it up and any little painting that there was wanting Addinal should do it as soon as it was ready that the smell might be gon off.*

Charlotte has got it all worked out in her own mind but it sounds to be more of a job than she thinks!

One hopes it was done to her liking for two years later history tragically repeated itself; on Wednesday morning 9th September 1767 Charlotte died two hours after giving birth to her first child, a stillborn daughter. Like her mother-in-law she had gone to her parents house for the birth and like her she was brought back to Burton Agnes to be buried. This time a dead baby came too.

Griffith remained a widower for less than a year. His new wife was Mary, daughter of James Hebblethwaite of Norton and the marriage took place at Burton Agnes on 1st August 1768. Her quickly ensuing pregnancy must have been an anxious time but all went well and a son and heir was born the following July, another little Griffith.

The Boyntons were a very fashionable couple, and sat for the most fashionable portrait painters of the day — at Burton Agnes there is a head-and-shoulders of Mary by Sir Joshua Reynolds, a larger one of her holding a baby painted by Richard Cosway in his lighter, almost impressionist style and full-length paintings of both by Francis Cotes grace the great Hall. Cotes was second only in reputation to Reynolds and would probably have inherited his mantle had the unfortunate fellow not died at the comparatively early age of 42 'choking on a soap cure for the stone'. In his canvasses we see Griffith gazing out of the window at his ancestral acres while showing off a fine pair of legs and Mary, very pretty in a beautiful dress of yellow silk and lace, standing in front of a vaguely classical landscape. Griffith was so impressed by this that on its completion he composed a love poem to his wife which is now displayed near it.

Griffith wished to be thought of as a cultured man. In his teens he had spent some time at Corpus Christi College, Cambridge, then known as Benet College, whose Master had been Dr. John Green, later Bishop of Lincoln and a friend of his father's. (Dr. Green wrote the memorial inscription to the fifth baronet in Burton Agnes church). The Cotes portrait shows Griffith holding a book and he became a Fellow of the Society of Antiquaries in London, one of the oldest of the learned societies and still going strong today. In practice, however, like most of his class, his life was given over to a round of pleasure. Society was much more mobile: improvements to the springing of carriages meant actual travel was more comfortable, especially for ladies, and so the season in London was followed by time spent at a watering place, and for the best people this meant Bath. Even the nobility, so long aloof from the gentry, patronised them and there was much more mixing between the two classes.

All towns of consequence had Assembly Rooms and Griffith was a subscriber to the York one. When they were first built earlier in the century the entertainment usually consisted of dancing followed by cards and refreshments, but by the 1760s dancing, card-playing and tea-drinking all went on at the same time and thus three rooms were required. People who wished to give similar entertainment in their own homes also required three rooms and in new houses these were arranged in a circular fashion on the first floor; old houses had to be adapted again. It seems that at Burton Agnes the third baronet's Saloon was given a new carved pine chimney piece and William Marlow, a young landscape painter based in York who had caught the fancy of the local gentry, painted picturesque scenes in the overdoor panels. To provide the other two rooms Sir Henry Griffith's large Withdrawing Room off it was divided and given delightful new plasterwork ceilings. So that one could circulate a new small flight of steps led through a doorway on to the half-landing of the main staircase.

Some new furniture was needed and that which Sir Griffith bought for the main room, an elegant suite of sofa, eight chairs and two window seats in the Hepplewhite style, their beechwood frames gessoed and painted white and gold, can still be seen there though the wood has been stripped.

Perhaps the most striking alterations to Burton Agnes at about this time were not in the house but in the garden where all the old planting, the parterres, the groves, the pallisades, the 'crooked Walkes' here, and in country house gardens generally, which required an army of gardeners to maintain, were swept away in favour of lawns with open vistas. So that this vista was uninterrupted, the animals in the park beyond, which were a necessary part of the view, were kept off the lawn by means of a 'ha-ha', described for the first time in John James' *The Theory and Practice of Gardening* published in 1712.

"At present we frequently make through views, called 'Ah, Ah', which are openings in the walls, without grilles, to the very level of the walks, with a large and deep ditch at the foot of them, lined on both sides to sustain the earth and prevent the getting over, which surprises the eye upon coming near it, and make one cry Ah! Ah! from whence it takes its name."

These original ha-has were short and used at the end of a gravel walk but now, as at Burton Agnes, they stretched the whole length of the new lawn, though in fact, as the considerable slope of the natural terrain had been levelled it was more of a retaining wall than a conventional ha-ha. It was also usual to put the wall on one side only with a slope on the other to prevent the animals falling in and being unable to get out.

In addition to the overdoor panels Sir Griffith commissioned four views from William Marlow. Three remain in the house, one showing the Boynton land towards the old town of Bridlington with Flamborough Head in the distance, one the old Manor House at Barmston and one the east side of Burton Agnes Hall then obviously considered to be the best elevation with its complete range of sash windows and extensive lawn bounded by the ha-ha. In 1985 the Bridlington and Barmston paintings went to the United States as part of the great "Treasure Houses of Britain" exhibition.

Standing in the Garden Gallery and looking towards the Bridlington Road one can see clumps of trees forming a sort of avenue. Tree clumps make one think of Capability Brown and certainly he was in the area at this time, advising Sir William Constable at Burton Constable. However Brown's clumps are usually arranged to reflect nature and these are in uncompromisingly straight lines suggesting that they were planted at a slightly earlier time, the time of the straight vistas, or maybe they were the first step in a new drive to the house, plans for which were subsequently abandoned.

In 1772 the death of the sitting MP for Beverley caused an unexpected by-election. None of the local families that had a traditional monopoly of the borough produced a candidate and, almost on a whim it seems, Sir Griffith decided to stand. Though unopposed until an hour before the poll the Beverley voters still expected to be bribed handsomely for their support and Griffith spent £966 5s. 6d. on getting himself elected. This accounted for most of the £1,000 he had borrowed from 'Mrs Boynton' (his aunt Adriana?) the previous November for the truth is that the free-spending lifestyle, the entertainment and entertaining in London, Bath and Burton Agnes, the portraits, the new furniture, the expensive clothes were all perched insecurely on a growing mountain of debt.

The account book kept by John Outram, Sir Griffith's steward, survives and shows that at the end of each financial year Sir Griffith borrowed money to balance his accounts. By 1771-2 Sir Griffith was in debt to a total of 17 people, usually at a rate of 4½% interest. Apart from the sale of a few animals and some tiles from his brickyard to his neighbour Constable his income was solely from his rents which were about £3,500. Generally speaking agricultural rents were rising at this time so there should have been no problem there. His taxes, which included land, window, coach, plate, constable, poor and church taxes remained more or less constant as did the wages he paid; what went up and up was the Boyntons' personal expenditure. Never had there been so many delightful things to spend money on and so many ways to waste it. It was a consumer society *par excellence*.

In that year Mary spent £439.10s. which included £100 allowed her 'on going to London' in October and the Boyntons remained away until April. Each month Sir Griffith sent home for more money; in November Outram sent £900 to London, in December £50 in two bank bills to Bath, in January £50 in two York Bank notes to London, in February £100 in two bills to London and in

Page from account book kept by John Outram, steward to the 6th Baronet detailing the latter's election expenses which include 'Expenses at 10 Publick Houses £54. 8s. 9d.'.

March a further £100 to London. In July Outram entered his own annual salary — £40 — and the interest he received on two loans of £50 and £600 he had made to his employer. Why he was prepared to lend him money when he knew better than anyone what the situation was remains a mystery and how, on a salary of £40 p.a., he had so much to lend another one though, as a Parliamentary Commissioner for land enclosures, he had at least one other source of income.

Sir Griffith was by no means alone in his financial situation nor was it all his fault. Griffith III had died in debt and the estate had had mortgages on it ever since as did those of most of the large landowners. This had semed to trouble them not at all but from now on many would face their come-uppance. Brought up to no other life than that of gentlemen of leisure, Griffith and his like carried on in the way they felt society expected them to, for they could not imagine what else to do and eventually one by one many went under.

Clever ones did survive and not always by marrying money though this was a common source of new income: the social round became secondary to the management of their estates which they took into their own hands. We are now in the age of Agrarian Revolution where the slow enclosure of the common

LIBRARY
BISHOP BURTON COLLEGE
BEVERLEY HU17 8QG

land and large fields with their strip farming, which had been going on for centuries, was dramatically speeded up. People with proper title to land now had a number of smaller compact fields of their own where they could put into practice the new ideas for crop and soil improvement. Those without lost out of course, but they were not the gentry.

Some landowners had lucky finds of minerals, but usually the ones who flourished were not the ancient families but relative upstarts like Sir Christopher Sykes who, while busily adding to the small estate at Sledmere that his family had inherited in the previous generation, improved, enclosed, planted and built a fine mansion, all again on borrowed money, but borrowed to make money, not just to keep going. His family origins were in trade and he brought financial acumen and new energy to the estate business, the very same qualities that Sir Henry Griffith and his contemporaries had had but which seemed to have been bred out of the following generations of ancient families.

Griffith had spent less and less time on his estate and the Burton Agnes fields were not enclosed until the middle of the next century, amongst the last in the country. Instead, at the same time as Christopher Sykes was buying, he started to dispose of his land, his capital asset, and of course as his acreage diminished, so did his rent. As the estate was still held under the terms of the second baronet's 'strict settlement' of 1661 a private Act of Parliament had to be obtained and this was passed in 1771. The possibility of his estate being dispersed from necessity rather than legal loopholes would never have entered Sir Francis's head.

Sir Griffith's rickety financial base could survive for his lifetime for people were usually happy to lend on a gentleman's bond as the interest was paid more or less on time but on 6th January 1778, while in London, Griffith died 'of a fever', leaving his eight year old son the new baronet, a baby, Francis, not yet a year and Mary six months pregnant with their third son. He owed over £24,000 on a private mortgage, bonds and contract debts and the unpaid costs of a Drainage Act.

The death of the sixth baronet marks the end of an era in the story of the Boynton family. There was to be no more involvement in national government and their standing in the county was much diminished. From now on they became local landowners of a shrinking estate and largely substituted country pursuits for high society. At the beginning of the present century a contemporary would write, 'the Boyntons lived for sport'.

CHAPTER NINE
FINANCIAL CRISES

George Parkhurst

Poor Lady Boynton, bereft of a loving husband and a glittering social life, left with huge debts and three boys to bring up and, under the terms of her husband's will, his sole executrix, was suddenly in a most unenviable position, and because the new baronet was a minor in law the position was even more complicated. Of course she had advisers and the first action was another Act of Parliament to enable her to sell a number of preferments to livings. For a long time right to appoint a clergyman had been considered another source of income to be bought and sold, the proprietor getting the money and the appointee a (smaller) stipend.

One way and another she struggled on. Though beautiful and charming, she was no catch for a prudent man and she must have been very lonely for what else could have possessed her to marry George Parkhurst? She could not have been unaware of his reputation. There is a hunting picture of 'Handsome Jack' as he was known (his first name was John) at Burton Agnes typically by Sawrey Gilpin, the well-known sporting and animal painter, charging through the

Signature of George Parkhurst on his marriage settlement with Mary, widow of sixth Baronet.

countryside with the hounds and, as the saying goes, handsome is as handsome does. With a gang of likeminded cronies he pursued one harebrained scheme after another and quickly went through his own money. Mary's marriage settlement dated 28th January 1784 and drawn up one feels by an anxious lawyer, allowed him one quarter of the Burton Agnes rents which was perhaps sufficient inducement for him but prevented his 'intermedling' with other Boynton assets such as Mary's jewellery and the plate, household goods and chattels left her by her husband. Where this is stated someone has underlined it heavily in pencil. George Parkhurst's confident, flamboyant hand at the bottom of the document is at least three times the size of any other family signature throughout the centuries.

He can therefore have been of little practical help to his wife who went on selling land to make ends meet. Moreover he was scarcely a suitable father substitute since he is recorded as bringing up his stepsons 'in every kind of vice.'

Sir Griffith Boynton, 7th Baronet 1769 — 1801

The younger two, who could not remember their father, seem to have survived in their own way but Griffith, the eldest, was certainly affected by this treatment. Described as a sweet-tempered youth he graduated from Trinity College Cambridge in 1789 and the following year married Anna Maria Parkhurst, daughter of Captain Richard Parkhurst. For a time he lived in Surrey, presumably to save money, and Burton Agnes must have been shut up, his mother, her husband and the younger boys going to live in Driffield, but he died at Burton Agnes in July 1801 aged 32. Burke's Peerage and Baronetage remarks,

> *"This gentleman, who was esteemed amongst the most accomplished of his time, totally secluded himself from society for several years before his death."*

There is a miniature of Griffith in the display case in the upstairs Drawing Room.

Sir Francis Boynton, 8th Baronet 1777 — 1832

Griffith had no children and so Francis, the second son, became the eighth baronet. A wild character, whose interests were confined mainly to blood sports, and totally reckless as far as money was concerned he was by far the greatest disaster in the fortunes of the Boyntons. He had tried one positive move as soon as he succeeded to the title; he attempted to exchange some land with the neighbouring St. Quintins the better to enclose the Burton Agnes fields only to discover that it had been the subject of a financial dispute never resolved and that ended the matter. By 1807 his borrowing and mortgaging had got him into such difficulty that his principal creditor, John Lockwood, a prominent Beverley man who made a fortune out of buying up property and mortgages but who seems genuinely to have tried to sort Francis out, appointed Henry John Shepherd, a young and able Beverley solicitor, to receive his rents and run the estate for one year. But the position proved pretty well intractable.

On the 8th March 1809 John Lockwood drew up a statement of the financial affairs of Sir Francis Boynton with some suggestions as to how matters might be ameliorated in time. A heavy charge on the estate were the portions of the two living Lady Boyntons. When they died the estate would be £3,000 better off. Mr. Lockwood estimated their ages to be about 60 (Mary) and between 40 and 50 (Anna Maria). He goes on to explain the current situation,

"Mr. Shepherd has already received one year's rents since Mr. Lockwood's deed of trust was executed but so far from their being any surplus to be applied in diminution of the £3,500 (the current debt) as proposed Mr. Lockwood has been under the necessity of advancing several sums of money at different times to prevent Sir Francis Boynton's being taken into confinement which sums amount to £3,000 for securing which an additional charge was made on the Estate by deed dated 27.1.1809."

This by no means satisfied the others involved who got together to demand action and a very sticky creditors' meeting followed. Henry Shepherd took the minutes. After Lockwood had given details of the position there was a long silence while he waited for the creditors to make a proposal; none was forthcoming. He then offered to arrange matters so that some of their principal was returned if they agreed not to declare Francis bankrupt and have him imprisoned. The minutes continue,

"To this after much Discussion they objected and at last gave their final determination not to give any Indulgence as to time ... nor to refrain from proceeding against Sir Francis unless some Person would then become answerable for payment for the whole of their demands at a future time."

Lockwood finally agreed to be that person and Francis was allowed £600 'for his Support and the payment of necessary salaries and incidental expenses.'

As readers of Jane Austen will know the correct answer to these problems was marriage to an heiress. Francis remained single for a further six years and then married Sally Bucktrout, the daughter of the landlord of the Black Swan Inn at York, and reputedly a former circus rider who, while in every other way no doubt a perfect partner for her husband, brought nothing more tangible with her than a reputation as a fearless horsewoman and is commemorated in contemporary hunting songs. The marriage settlement, significantly drawn up after the wedding, is concerned solely with the arrangements for her maintenance after her husband's death, a further charge on the estate, but inescapable. Her signature at the bottom is cramped and scratched with a large blot on the 'Y' of Sally.

This year, 1815, also saw the death of his mother; described as Mary Parkhurst, wife of John George Parkhurst of Catesby, her will was granted probate on 11th September. Perhaps the removal of the necessity to pay his mother's pension led Francis into wedlock.

Francis never mended his ways and his wife was no help. Amongst the legal documents is the draft of a plaintive letter dated 10th February 1832 (the year Francis died) to Sally Boynton from Henry Shepherd, who must by then have taken over the responsibility for Francis's finances and be wishing he hadn't.

Signature of Sir Francis Boynton and Sally Boynton (née Bucktrout)
on their marriage settlement.

"....you will see what strong grounds I have for frequently urging upon Sir Francis the insufficiency of the rents to meet the charges and the impossibility of my making any further advance. ...
The annual loss falls upon myself and it is calculated to be the ruin of myself and my family as well as being highly ruinous to Sir Francis. ...
You are quite mistaken, if you suppose that I am possessed of property to make these matters unimportant. It is quite out of my power to advance you the £25 you want even for so desirable an object as you mention."

Sally Boynton's portrait by H. B. Chalon shows a lady of no great beauty, mounted and dressed in hunting habit. Chalon, then quite fashionable, is also responsible for the rest of the paintings that remain from Francis's time and it seems wholly appropriate that they are all of animals, a small study of fearsome dogs and three large paintings of pairs of horses with not only tails but ears cropped in the horrible fashion then current. It is said that Sir Francis bred these horses for George III. One of the paintings includes a number of fighting cocks, part of a famous breed kept by Sir Francis; the cockpit he had dug can still be seen in Park Field beyond the lawn. It is interesting that they were able to find the money for paintings, horses and gamecocks. The only portrait in the house of Francis is as a young boy.

After her husband's death Lady Boynton went on to marry Sir Walter Strickland so she must have had something; her annuity perhaps.

CHAPTER TEN
FINANCIAL RECOVERY AND ARCHITECTURAL DISASTER

Sir Henry Griffith, 9th Baronet 1778 — 1854

Francis was also childless so on his death in 1832 the third brother Henry, at that point living at Haisthorpe Hall, became the ninth baronet and owner of Burton Agnes Hall. Quite different from Griffith and Francis, Henry was a family man having ten children by his wife Mary Gray, daughter of Captain Gray of Dover, whom he married in 1810. Miss Gray brought a fortune to the Boyntons (had her father made his money in the Napoleonic Wars?) and improved the position considerably.

This was the largest family that the house had had to accommodate; it had to be adapted again and probably at this time the two entertaining rooms made out of the Jacobean Withdrawing Room became bedrooms.

Having been thought of as 'barbaric' throughout the Georgian period there was now a resurgence of interest in Tudor and Stuart architecture and in 1832 Ackerman's of New Bond Street London published *The Architectural Remains of the reigns of Elizabeth and James I. From accurate drawings and measurements taken from existing Specimens by Charles James Richardson, F.R.I.B.A.* In it are several examples from Burton Agnes including the fireplace and part of the ceiling of the Long Gallery, and, with one small exception (see illustration on page 104) drawn with meticulous accuracy. In the accompanying text Richardson gives detailed measurements of the flowers and foliage — in case anyone should wish to reproduce them in papier maché — and the following description:-

> *"with its ceiling painted in appropriate colours, (it) presented an enlarged model of one of those bowers or walls of arched trellis-work, covered with shrubs, so common in the gardens of the time ... some of the leaves are used separately and made to hang down, the whole producing a good effect."*

It must have been shortly afterwards that the ceiling collapsed. Now that there was money available for repairs the leaky old tiled roof was replaced with slate and that may have been the last straw for a structure weakened by years of damp. In due course good use was made of a large part of the space; no-one now needed a Long Gallery but the house was very short of proper accommodation for maids and so seven small rooms with stoothing-wall partitions and a false ceiling were inserted with access from the back stairs. The large room off the west end of the gallery was used, as before, as the nursery. The rest, about a third of the original, and the room off it, were left to become ever more derelict and dusty.

1841 saw the beginning of the 10-yearly population census which gives us fascinating insights into the households of the time. In 1851, for instance, the

Boyntons' consisted of Sir Henry and Lady Boynton and Mary an unmarried daughter aged 40. To look after them were 10 servants headed by James Elliott, butler, and Elizabeth Smith and Susan Harrison, lady's maids, and including the cook, washermaid, groom, gardener and rather mysteriously, one agricultural servant and two agricultural labourers, all described as living in the house. The groom was deaf — various disabilities had to be recorded. This is a good sized establishment, indicative of the revival of the Boynton fortunes.

Sir Henry lived to be 76 having had 22 years as owner of Burton Agnes Hall, not bad for a third son. There are two portraits of him at Burton Agnes, a very good one of him as a young man and a further one in middle age.

Sir Henry Boynton, 9th Baronet.

Sir Henry Boynton, 10th Baronet.

CHAPTER ELEVEN
THE VICTORIAN AND EDWARDIAN HOUSE

Sir Henry Boynton, 10th Baronet 1811 — 1869

Not only must his eldest son Henry have been giving considerable thought to what he would do once he got his hands on the old house he also had the money to carry it out. The sale of land along the line of the Hull to Bridlington railway opened in 1846, would have brought in a useful amount to the estate but he had also done the proper thing and married it — twice.

His first wife Louisa, daughter of Walter Strickland of Cokethorpe Park, died in 1841 without children but left him £4,948 7s. 3d. Two years later he did even better. His new wife was Harriet Susannah Lightfoot, the daughter of Thomas Lightfoot of Old Burlington Street, London, a very wealthy man. The draft of their marriage settlement carefully drawn up by the bride's family firm of Lightfoot, Robson and Lightfoot and annotated by Henry's lawyer, who went through it with a toothcomb, shows that the Boynton side contributed not a penny. The first item is £1,000 cash for Henry immediately after the wedding plus £100 each year for life and it goes on in like vein including detailed provision for the children of the marriage. Mr. Lightfoot was prepared to go to considerable lengths to convert Miss Lightfoot, then aged 31, into Lady Boynton.

This view may, of course, be completely unfounded and Henry and Harriet have fallen in love.

One wonders what a young lady from London made of country life in East Yorkshire. At first the couple lived at Burton Agnes where their son Henry Somerville was born the following year. They then moved to 'Fort House' Bridlington, now the Barclay's Bank building in Manor Street. The area round Bridlington Quay was becoming a fashionable development since sea-bathing had become popular and younger branches of several county families had houses there. A daughter, Katherine Maude, was born in 1847 and this completed their family. In the 1851 census Henry's occupation is given as 'magistrate' and they have five servants, butler, cook, lady's maid, housemaid and nurse.

Henry senior was very interested in his family history, hence the 'Somerville' harking back to the glory days of the 14th century. On his first wife's death he had a hatchment made — the lozenge shaped coat of arms which was attached to the house after a death and then transported to the church on the bier — and left instructions for another on his own death. Both hang in Burton Agnes church, the last of the collection there as the custom now died out.

When Henry's father died in 1854 they moved to the big house and both set to work. Being a Boynton one of Henry's first actions was to rebuild the stables with good accommodation for the coachmen and grooms above. Meanwhile

Harriet looked at the furniture and, not liking what she saw, in the course of time practically refurnished the place out of her own pocket. No doubt she brought quite a lot with her from Bridlington.

As for the house itself the pendulum of taste had swung right back. 18th century classicism was out, denegrated as 'flat and insipid'; the Victorians borrowed avidly from all previous styles and new houses might have Norman keeps, medieval Great Halls, Gothic windows, battlements, anything and everything. How lucky for the Boyntons that previous generations had not had the inclination or the money to re-do the house completely — where others were putting up pastiches they had the genuine article. Sir Henry Griffith's Low Dining Room was now bang up to date, the panelling regilded and repainted with the monogram H B in various places it became the Drawing Room, quite a formal place where Lady Boynton received other ladies making morning calls in their carriages and dispensed tea at five o'clock to both sexes. This additional meal was necessary as the hour for dinner, probably about 11 am in old Sir Henry Griffith's time, had got progressively later through the centuries until it

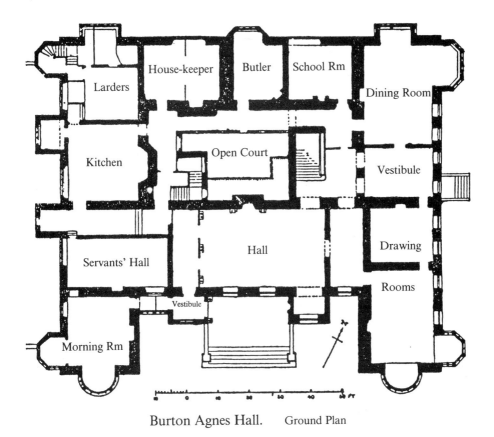

Burton Agnes Hall.   Ground Plan

Burton Agnes Hall:
plan of ground floor showing Victorian arrangement of rooms.

95

was now often 8 pm. The Chinese Room was also used as a Drawing Room but for some reason called the Japan Room, perhaps because the black background of the screens tied up with the vogue for covering things with black lacquer, known as 'japanning'.

The old Still Room was now the Dining Room, its walls covered with redundant panelling from the Long Gallery, the magnificently carved chimney piece reduced by two panels to fit. The big room upstairs had been transformed into the Ballroom.

The Victorians felt it a moral duty to provide properly for their servants —and to keep the sexes apart, hence the rooms in the Long Gallery for the maids. The cellar stairs leading out of the old Buttery were done away with and it and the space beyond were made into the Servants' Hall with a long row of bells, connecting to the various rooms by the usual ingenious arrangement of levers and pulleys, hung high on the passage wall opposite the door. The Kitchen was left where it was despite being a long way from the Dining Room. It was important to keep the smells from the rest of the house and hot cupboards were usually provided in Dining Rooms. The Pantry and Bakehouse were now larders but out of them still led the staircase to the rooms in the attic for male staff. The Wash-house, which had long lost its original function, was divided into two and became the housekeeper's domain and finally half of the Chapel became the Butler's Pantry and the other half was taken over by the family and became the School room (girls being educated at home by a governess, boys joining them until they went away to school). The old place, which had never adapted very happily to the needs of the Georgians now worked surprisingly well as a Victorian establishment.

Given their liking for everything ancient it seems odd that the Victorians became over-impressed by the invention of plate-glass and here and in houses large and small throughout the country huge sheets of it replaced small window-panes. They were certainly easier to clean though that can scarcely have been the reason.

In 1852, seven years after his marriage, but before he succeeded to the baronetcy, Henry was made a deputy Lord Lieutenant. He and his wife had completed the restoration of the family reputation and with it the Boyntons rightful place in the county community which they continued to fill for the rest of their lives. Henry died at the age of 58 after a fall from his horse: there is a small unnamed portrait of him hanging in the Hall.

Sir Henry Somerville Boynton, 11th Baronet 1844 — 1899

The next and last Sir Henry went to Magdalen College, Cambridge, and succeeded his father in July 1869 aged 25. At the age of 32 he married Mildred Augusta Paget, daughter of the Rev. Thomas Bradley Paget, vicar of Welton, and their only child, Cycely Mabel, was born the following year. Mildred became a keen follower of the Holderness Hunt.

There was very little alteration in the household arrangements. On the night of the 1881 census Sir Henry was the only member of the family at home, his wife and little daughter being away on a visit and presumably accompanied by a lady's maid and nurse but in the house were the butler, footman, cook, housemaid and two under housemaids though the agricultural labourers of 1851 have gone. Ten years on all three Boyntons were in residence and an interesting addition to the staff is Fraulein Selina von Lengefeld, 13-year-old Cycely's German governesss, whose place of birth is given as Pomerania.

Also interesting is how far from home upper servants were prepared to travel for suitables places; the lady's maid came from Worksop, the footman from Market Drayton and the housekeeper from the Isle of Man.

The inventory made on Sir Henry's death in 1899, of all the contents of Burton Agnes Hall taken by James Elwell, head of the famous Beverley woodworking firm, but here wearing his less familiar hat as valuer, presents a vivid picture of the interior of a Victorian country house, crowded with furniture, paintings, and bric-a-brac.

The Great Hall for instance was now the Saloon, the name used in many country houses of the period for the general sitting room, the Screen openings filled by 'doors' of red brocade stretched over frames. The floor was covered with red felt and over this was a Turkey carpet 20' by 15'. It made a sizeable room but nevertheless in it were 25 chairs some of which were large overstuffed armchairs, 2 sofas, a large centre ottoman and an s-shaped 'conversational stool'. There were also numerous tables of different sizes and various other pieces. The alcove was fitted out as a writing area with desk, chairs and a large number of writing implements. The drawing room was just as full and had net curtains at the windows.

The stairs were carpeted with crimson felt drugget held by brass stair-rods. Cycely's bedroom contained a French bedstead with cretonne draperies and spring and hair mattresses (very up-to-date) and a feather bolster and pillows. Somewhat in contrast to this femininity the walls were hung with a quantity of small sporting engravings. Cycely also had a birch writing table and various chairs and in her dressing room was a birch wash table with marble slab, a pink and cream toilet set with chamber pot, and a hip bath and rug. All the bedrooms in the house, including the state bedrooms, contained similar toilet articles and hip baths.

Since the death of Lady Harriet Boynton in 1889 about half the furniture in the house had belonged to Cycely; bought by Harriet it had remained there when she moved out on the death of her husband and she had left it all to her grand-daughter.

But nothing in the Ballroom, the most amazing room in the house, had been hers. The usual hunting and shooting Boynton, Sir Henry also kept falcons and was a great fisherman, spending part of each year in Norway for the purpose, but his great passion was Natural History which he indulged to the full turning the Ballroom into a museum. Against each wall were glass cases of various sizes containing stuffed birds, usually in pairs but some singly and some in groups, sheldrake, widgeon, goosander, nightjar, bittern etc. etc. Elwell counted all the cases: 20 on the south side, 25 on the east, 22 on the north and 104 on the west, the chimney wall. On a table in the middle were a further 12 and there were 23 more in the north window making a grand total of 206. Also in the window were a stuffed water rat, weasel and trout, and the hand of a mummy while in the 'oriel' window were various bits and pieces including a mammoth tusk and tooth, 6 pairs of thigh bones (unidentified) and a fossilised turnip.

Some other items not usually associated with a natural history collection had found their way into the ballroom — a quantity of toys, a pair of snow shoes, two broken vases, a bicycle and an oak bidet and pan. Hard luck if Lady Boynton had ever entertained thoughts of launching Cycely with a Coming-Out Ball at Burton Agnes.

This was not all by any means. In the 1880s the old Steward's Room with the Plate House removed had been taken into family use as the owner's office, panelled with some rather good stuff — where from? — and connected to the entrance lobby with a new short corridor. In this passage were the large head of a Norwegian Elk (killed 26th September 1893), a stuffed badger, two otters and three polecoats while in the office, not only were there two cases of stuffed birds but also three cages of live ones, a small indication of what was to be found outside where Collier (see below) says "there are several acres covered with bird cages containing birds spending their lives in luxurious captivity".

After Sir Henry's death the specimens in glass cases were sent to Hull Museum and were bombed in 1942. There is no record of what happened to the live ones.

Somehow Sir Henry also found time to be a JP but he did not seek election to the new East Riding County Council, nor did any of his successors. Formed as a result of the Local Government Act of 1888 its first Chairman, Mr. David Burton of Cherry Burton, remarked,

"It virtually marked the close of the old feudal form of county government, and the transference of the government from a privileged class to the representatives of the county".

So it did, in time, but to contemporaries it hardly looked like that since, with the exception of one or two like Sir Henry, pretty well all those elected were the landed proprietors who had done the job before. Which tenants in 1889 were not going to vote for their landlord?

There is no portrait of the last Sir Henry on display at Burton Agnes but there is one of Mildred, a rather sweet faced lady who was 'esteemed for many kindly qualities'.

CHAPTER TWELVE
THE TWENTIETH CENTURY

Mrs. Cycely Wickham-Boynton 1877 — 1947

On Sir Henry's death the title went to his cousin and then to his cousin's son who became the thirteenth Baronet, but thirteen was an unlucky number for one of the oldest baronetcies in England and it became extinct on his death in 1966. Under the historic family arrangements Sir Henry was obliged to leave the house to his titular heir but all the rest of the property went to his daughter and she remained in the house paying rent to Sir Griffith.

Sir Henry died just before Cycely's 22nd birthday. Seven months later, in Burton Agnes Church, she married Thomas Lamplugh Wickham JP of Chestnut Grove, Boston Spa, whereupon they hyphenated their names ('by wish of her father') and became Captain and Mrs. Wickham-Boynton. They had two sons, Henry, born in 1900 and Marcus, born 1904.

Being female did not make Cycely any less a Boynton; she loved the outdoor life and was a particularly fine horsewoman. This interest was fully shared by her husband who was master of the Middleton Hunt for many years and set up the Burton Agnes Stud Farm to become one of the country's foremost breeders of hunters winning many of the Hunter Improvement Society's awards.

Cycely was also concerned with the Girl Guide movement, holding rallies at Burton Agnes which from time to time were attended by Queen Mary, consort of George V — at last a Royal Visit!

In 1910 Sydney White painted full length portraits of the Wickham-Boyntons and there is also one of 17-year-old Cycely by Baumann painted at the same time as that of her mother.

The Wickham-Boyntons were both keen on their ancestry. The Wickhams claimed descent from William Wickham (1539-1595) successively Bishop of Lincoln and Bishop of Winchester. This leads to confusion with the earlier more famous bishop, William of Wykeham (1324-1404), founder of New College and Winchester School and indeed there was a long-running but futile legal battle in the 17th century attempting to establish kinship with the latter which would enhance the standing of the Wickham family and also enable their sons to be admitted free to his school, though any saving would have quickly been swallowed up by the enormous costs of the litigation.

In his time this was blocked by Lord Saye and Sele who indubitably was a descendant. Thus the family were not able to use the Wykeham coat of arms of three roses and chevron though they did appropriate the famous motto 'Manners Makyth Man' and the bull's head emblem, both of which can be seen in the house. Characteristically, on her husband's death, Cycely Wickham-Boynton pursued the matter of the roses and chevron and eventually got permission to include it in the coat of arms on his memorial tablet in Burton

Cycely Wickham-Boynton with Sir Griffith Boynton, 13th Baronet,
and his wife Naomi.

Meeting of the Middleton Hunt:
l. to r. Cycely Wickham-Boynton, Thomas Wickham-Boynton
and Henry Wickham-Boynton.

Agnes Church. There is a portrait of William Wickham, who preached the sermon at the funeral of Mary, Queen of Scots, in Burton Agnes Hall.

There was an account of the Wickham family in print, largely given over to a detailed account of this dispute, but none of the Boyntons and after an initial attempt to write one with the help of the Rev. Carus Vale Collier, then curate of Burton Agnes, Thomas Wickham-Boynton passed the whole job over to him and it is from his account, based on painstaking research, and access to the many old documents and deeds then stored in the Long Gallery that much of our present knowledge of the family comes.

Unfortunately Cycely was less interested in the house. To begin with she had certainly made some alterations and improvements. After her father's museum had been dismantled she turned the Victorian Ballroom into a Drawing Room, collecting up and reinstalling the Hepplewhite suite, dispersed around the house while it was out of fashion, and her father's office, known as the Oak Room became her Morning Room, but otherwise she seems to have left most of the rooms as they were, complete with Victorian clutter. When electricity came to the village she put in electric lighting and bells and partial central heating was installed using vast, ornate radiators and pipes of large diameter. She had all the plate glass replaced by small-pane windows which considerably improved the appearance of the house. Her idea of painting the panelling in the Great Hall cream was a less happy one.

Though there was now a reasonable water supply the only bathroom was one installed by her son Henry at his own expense and for his own use. A professional soldier who rose to the rank of major he had his own income and wanted more comfort when he came home on leave. Water was now pumped up from the village pond; until that was achieved it had still been supplied from the well though latterly pumped, (the old bucket is in front of the café, filled with flowers) and led by conduit into the house. But as time went on she spent less and less money on the house and it began once more to fall into disrepair.

When the Second World War broke out in 1939 both Wickham-Boynton sons were involved and Mrs. Wickham-Boynton was devastated when Henry, her heir and by far her favourite child, came back to Burton Agnes in 1942 to die of an illness caught while on active service with the Scots Greys. This was followed by the death of her husband later the same year. Now there was only Marcus left and he would inherit. Born, so the story goes, at the end of a hard day's hunting, he always seems to have been an irritation to his mother who had little time for him. Stories abound in the village of him as a young boy doing odd jobs for her tenants in order to earn some money to spend in the village shop.

However, he could not escape the inbred love of horses and after Eton and Sandhurst went to France to work at what is now the Headquarters of the French National Stud. This was followed by a spell as Junior Assistant to the famous trainer Atty Pearse and then ten years at Lord Carnarvon's Highclere Stud where he was both Stud Manager and Estate Manager.

It was during this time he developed the interest in paintings, particularly French Impressionist and Post-Impressionist, that became one of the ruling passions of his life and started the collection that is such an important feature of the house today.

After the war, when he served in the Welsh Guards, he came back to Burton Agnes to prepare for his eventual take-over but relations with his mother were no better. Dinner over, she would sit in the Morning Room while he furnished the Chinese Room with a comfortable three piece suite and remained there. Eventually he decided to do up the old Rectory for himself but before it was ready to move into Cycely Wickham-Boynton died on 27th February 1947. "Well, that's it then," said Marcus.

Marcus Wickham-Boynton 1904 — 1989

Marcus's behaviour at this point would be of interest to a psychologist. Immediately after his mother's funeral he got rid of all her personal belongings, throwing many of them out of her bedroom window. Her jewellery he sold. Next to go were the family papers, some were sold but many were burnt, which action he probably later regretted, though not as much as the writer. Feeling that his mother had spent an inordinate amount of money on her hunters that should have been put to better use they all went, too.

Alterations to the inheritance laws meant that he could now buy the house from his cousin. The combination of his mother's general neglect and war restrictions had left it in a very sad way and it needed much money spent on it. The war had virtually put an end to the hunter Stud and anyway, hunters were out as far as Marcus was concerned. Realising that the future was in racehorses he reorganised the business with great success concentrating on breeding yearlings which fetched high prices at the Newmarket sales, the proceeds he spent on the house and contents.

Having made sure the place was watertight and not likely to fall down Marcus Wickham-Boynton instigated a scheme of refurbishment and refurnishing that went on for the rest of his long life. "You must always have plans", he said. The cream paint in the Great Hall was stripped off and the oak panelling there and in the King's and Queen's rooms cleaned and given a yearly treatment with linseed oil until it could take no more. The dining room panelling was replaced by red silk wall covering and a white dado, the chimney piece remaining. A more fundamental change was the re-siting of the kitchen to the old Schoolroom next door the the Dining Room (originally half the chapel) which was lined with modern cupboards in a fairly awful pink formica — a rare lapse of taste if it was Marcus's choice.

Most of the furniture — Harriet Boynton's legacy — was not to his liking, moderate old oak stuff he called it and in time about 90% of it was replaced. This was no hardship. He actively enjoyed buying and selling, especially if he could talk his way into a bargain. In another incarnation he would have enjoyed being a dealer. Those pieces that remain include the oak draw-leaf table in the Great Hall, the magnificent 17th century Nonesuch Chest, the William and Mary chairs in the King's and Queen's rooms and of course the suite in the upstairs Drawing Room.

The long table in the Great Hall came from the Delamere family home in Cheshire. The second Lord Delamere had been a school friend of Marcus and in the 1950s he went to visit them in Kenya where they now lived. He was very taken with the life there and ended up buying a 100,000 acre ranch, 'Ol Pejeta', where he spent the winters for several years. At first he stocked it with sheep but when this proved not a good idea as the wool caught in the thorn bushes they were replaced by cattle, at one time numbering 11,000 head.

In 1961 Snr. Vicente Arroyo came to Burton Agnes as a secretary/assistant to Marcus Wickham-Boynton. Over the years he became an indispensible friend and companion and was a great help with the restoration of the house and the building up of the collection which now included works by Renoir, Matisse, Utrillo and many other famous names. The collection was not static — if the market was right he would sell and buy something else that took his fancy. Other things came and went besides paintings — at one time there was a rather good display of Lucie Rie and Bernard Leach pottery that is there no longer. He widened his interests to take in Chinese Ceramics and bronzes, there are two important ones by Epstein and several by living artists including Sally Arnup.

He also kept an eye open for family portraits that came on the market; in this way, amongst others, the Cosway Mary Hebblethwaite and the Gilpin John Parkhurst came to Burton Agnes. The very fine 'Ravenscroft Boys' by Philip Reinagle which was highly praised when it was exhibited at the Royal Academy in 1819 came to the family because a niece of theirs married a Wickham.

Early on, in 1949, he decided to let the house earn some of its own living by opening part of it to the paying public. Houses had always been accessible to the respectable visitor who would be shown round by the housekeeper as Elizabeth Bennett was shown round Pemberley in *Pride and Prejudice*, but to let all and sundry in on purchase of a ticket was a new idea resorted to by hard-pressed owners faced with making good wartime neglect and damage and reeling under the new death duties — the Wickham-Boyntons had had to pay two lots in five years. After a very tentative start of three afternoons a week, for who knew what interest there would be, it has been a great success and is now open every day from 1st April to 31st October and attracts 30,000 visitors a year.

From time to time further adjustments were made 'behind the scenes'. In 1938 mains water had finally come to Burton Agnes and Marcus Wickham-Boynton eventually had all the bedrooms provided with bathrooms. He also installed full central heating. Self-contained 'flats' now provide accommodation for live-in staff and ladies from the village come in each morning to clean right through the house. The garden was not neglected, a colourful shrubbery was planted to the north of the lawn and the pond dug in three stages and so cleverly designed that it seems to have been there forever. A touch of personal luxury was the building of an indoor swimming pool disguised as an orangery.

Marcus Wickham-Boynton's greatest achievement, however, was the restoration of the Long Gallery. The derelict east end was tackled first, in 1951, and from one small remaining piece of the original ceiling and the Richardson illustrations the architect, Francis Johnson of Bridlington, who has been associated with the house for over 50 years, was able to design a panel of four rose trails which he hoped would 'hang together without looking mechanical'. These panels were cast flat in fibrous plaster which assumed the barrel shape of the original ceiling when fixed to battens. The architect and the owner were both proud of the fact that the work was done by Yorkshire craftsmen, Smallwoods of Bridlington the builders and Taylor and Salter of Leeds the plasterers. At the

*Charles Richardson's drawing of the original ceiling and fireplace
in the Long Gallery (the three centre panels,
now forming the Dining Room chimney piece).
He corrected the spelling of Hoope.*

same time the room off, known as the Library, was restored, first putting back the dividing wall though one option had been to leave the whole area open. No attempt was made to replace the oak panelling, instead the walls were given a low dado and painted, a simple treatment which showed to advantage the part of the art collection that now hung there, and was sympathetic in period with the doors and door frames salvaged from nearby Kilnwick Hall, sadly demolished in the same year. To complete the scheme the cornice and frieze were copied exactly from one at Kilnwick and the library cornice was another copy, of one made in 1749 by Thomas Perritt of York.

It was 23 years before the rest of the Long Gallery was restored. Besides being twice as long as the first section all the Victorian maids' rooms had to be swept away; the west Palladian window was temporarily removed, out through the space went the old walls and ceilings and in came the new panels. This time the builders were another Bridlington firm, Gants, and the plasterers Steads of Bradford. The gallery also acquired two new windows, those at each end of the south wall and to complete the scheme a magnificent fireplace of sculpture and Siena marbles, previously in the ballroom of another demolished house, Methley Hall near Leeds, was installed.

The grand undertaking was now finished. Whilst not attempting to copy nature as exactly as the original ceiling of which similar plasterwork can still be seem on the end walls, its deep undercutting made possible by the painstaking building up of each flower petal by petal, a process prodigal of time and labour and prohibitively expensive nowadays unless one is a millionaire and restoring Spencer House, the ceiling is undoubtedly an enormous sucess. A happy thought was to make it 'inhabited', principally with goats, the emblem of the Boyntons, of which there are ten but there are seven other creatures to be found, to the especial delight of younger visitors, and the initials of the people who worked on the Gallery are also there together with those of Marcus William Wickham-Boynton.

The Kilnwick salvage included the Tudor oak linenfold (or, more strictly, parchment-fold, since its design reflects the spines of old books) panelling from the old court room which featured a series of carved heads and two interesting coats-of-arms, an early one of Henry VIII, with his first wife Queen Catherine of Aragon's pomegranate emblem, and one of the Percy family, Earls of Northumberland. There had always been speculation that this panelling might have come from Leconfield Castle, the Percys' great house referred to earlier, demolished and much of the contents sold in 1610 by the then earl. Keen to preserve this bit of Yorkshire history Mr. Wickham-Boynton bought the panelling and had it installed in the State Guest Apartment ante-room which became known as the Justices' Room. Unfortunately there was not quite enough and some patching with new wood was necessary. The resulting piebald appearance of the room grated on Mr. Wickham-Boynton and eventually he had all the panelling painted, which grates on many visitors.

Marcus Wickham-Boynton's public life reflected his interests: he was Steward of Beverley Racecourse for several years but he had also been a JP,

Restoration of the Long Gallery and Library:
architect's drawing by Francis Johnson & Partners
showing alternative treatment with no replacement of wall between.

The Library:
restoration as carried out with wall replaced.

Deputy-Lieutenant of the East Riding and was High Sheriff of Yorkshire in 1953, the year Queen Elizabeth II was crowned. His framed Command to be present at the coronation hangs in the downstairs Drawing Room and the stool he sat on in Westminster Abbey is in the Chinese Room. Companion portraits of him and his brother Henry (the latter painted posthumously) by David Jagger can also be seen.

He died in December 1989 at the age of 85. A man whom some found difficult, he was nevertheless genuinely mourned by many. He was buried in the family vault in Burton Agnes churchyard, he had personally inspected it to make sure there was room, but his true memorial is Burton Agnes Hall. In an age when the political and economic climate meant little or no assistance was available and many owners of historic properties gave up the struggle so that, like Kilnwick Hall, they were pulled down or allowed to decay, he and his house triumphed.

The Cunliffe-Listers

After more than three centuries of ownership the Boyntons had gone. Very much aware that he was the last of his line Marcus Wickham-Boynton had thought long about the future of Burton Agnes Hall which he wanted preserved with its contents intact. After a flirtation with the National Trust, whose proposals did not meet with his requirements, he formed in 1977 a private Trust dedicated to the house and 42 acres of surrounding gardens and grounds which he endowed with money and 600 acres of the estate.

But an essential part of the charm of Burton Agnes is that all its life it has remained a family home and who was going to live there and inherit the estate? Mr. Wickham-Boynton eventually settled on the Cunliffe-Lister family who like him are direct descendants of the ninth baronet.

In 1886 the Rev. Charles Boynton, rector of Barmston, grandson of the ninth baronet, cousin of the 11th and brother of the 12th, married Mary Constance Cunliffe-Lister, daughter of Samuel Cunliffe-Lister. The family seat was at Manningham near Bradford but his father was a manufacturer and politician becoming Bradford's first MP after the 1832 Reform Bill.

Samuel Cunliffe-Lister was the founder of Listers, the famous cloth manufacturers. Possessed of enormous energy he declined a proposed career in the church and served an apprenticeship with Sands, Turner and Co. merchants of Liverpool, in whose employ he crossed the Atlantic six times (by sail) before he was 21, then persuaded his father to provide the finance for a steam-powered worsted spinning mill. Having seen the Boyntons fail to take advantage of the Agrarian Revolution we now have a man who grasped the possibilities of the following Industrial Revolution with both hands.

He was a brilliant inventor and over the years took out more than 150 patents. He was the first person to produce a machine to comb the fine botany wool by power; he then spent 10 years developing a way of putting silk waste to profitable use. This led to the buying of silk-growing estates in India and eventually to the production of silk velvet. After a disastrous fire at his mills in 1871 he built new ones covering 27 acres which remained the core of the Lister mills. He was a great benefactor to Bradford; his house and grounds, which the corporation acquired from him was renamed Lister Park and a statue of him erected.

He was very concerned that the government's Free Trade policy was adversely affecting home industries and with Lord William Bentinck founded the Fair-Trade League, writing many pamphlets in support of it.

At the age of 68 he spent nearly £1,000,000 buying the Swinton Park, Jervaulx and Middleham Castle estates in North Yorkshire and went back to his roots as a country landowner of great benevolence. In 1891 he was granted a peerage with the title Lord Masham which he took from the small market town. He kept his abilities until the end dying in 1906 at the age of 92. In 1905 he had published *Lord Masham's Inventions*.

Though he had had a large family of two sons and five daughters his only surviving grandchild was the daughter of Mary Constance Boynton, also Mary and now the wife of Sir Philip Lloyd-Greame of Sewerby Park, Bridlington. She therefore inherited the Swinton estates and she and her husband adopted her grandfather's name. Sir Philip Cunliffe-Lister, as he now was, had entered parliament and became successively President of the Board of Trade and Colonial Secretary when he was created Viscount Swinton.

During the Second World War tragedy hit when John the elder of their two sons was killed in the North African campaign himself leaving two small sons. On the death of their grandmother in 1974, much lamented by her tenants to whom she had been friend as well as landlord, the elder, David, became the second earl. His wife is the well-known life-peer Baroness Masham who, wheel-chair bound from a riding accident, works hard for disabled people.

Nicholas, the younger son, a solicitor, married Susan Whitelaw, the eldest of the four daughters of Lord (William) Whitelaw, the former Deputy Prime-Minister. They have three children, Lorna, Mark and Simon and it will be Simon who will take over the responsibility for Burton Agnes Hall in 2002 when he is 25 (his elder brother is heir to his uncle).

In the meantime his mother is in charge. A keen practical gardener with a real flair for garden design she has transformed the walled garden. Whilst keeping part for its original function as a provider of fruit and vegetables for the house, the latter now grown in a decorative 'potager', she has planted many flowers and shrubs, including over 200 varieties of her favourite campanulas and, to the delight of children of all ages, has also introduced a maze with a brainteaser in the middle together with several outdoor games including giant chess and Snakes and Ladders each in its single-colour flower plot.

In the house one much appreciated alteration has been the conversion of the room off the west end of the Long Gallery, formerly a guest bedroom and at one time the night nursery, into a delightful sitting room where people can rest and browse through books on the painters whose work is displayed in the house. Soft-furnishing being another of her talents she made the curtains and re-covered the sofa and easy chair. There are also various examples of her tapestry work in the house, notably a cushion in the Queen's Room based on

the honeysuckle ceiling design. Informal family snapshots are also appearing.

Susan Cunliffe-Lister's touch is again seen in the many vases of fresh flowers, dried arrangements and bowls of sweet-smelling pot-pourri, all her work from the produce of the garden, which bring colour and life to the rooms. Pot plants also abound, a speciality of the head gardener who maintains the greenhouses, gardens and ground with one other full-time and occasional part-time staff — and Mrs. Cunliffe-Lister.

LIBRARY
BISHOP BURTON COLLEGE
BEVERLEY HU17 8QG

FAMILY TREE OF THE OWNERS OF THE BURTON AGNES MANOR HOUSES

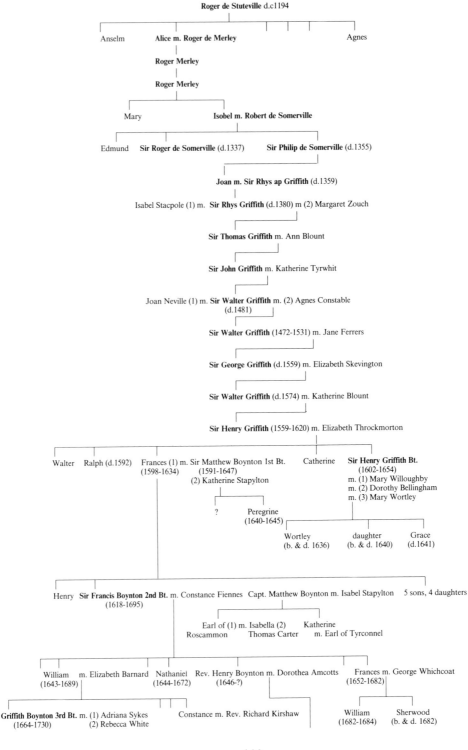

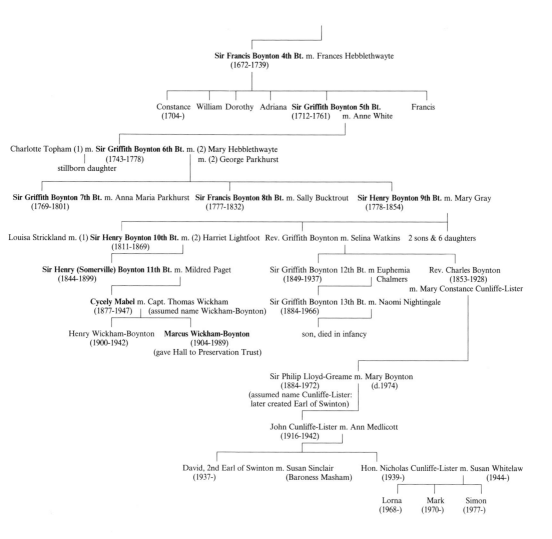

Sir Francis Boynton 4th Bt. m. Frances Hebblethwayte
(1672-1739)

Constance William Dorothy Adriana **Sir Griffith Boynton 5th Bt.** Francis
(1704-) (1712-1761) m. Anne White

Charlotte Topham (1) m. **Sir Griffith Boynton 6th Bt.** m. (2) Mary Hebblethwayte
(1743-1778) m. (2) George Parkhurst
stillborn daughter

Sir Griffith Boynton 7th Bt. m. Anna Maria Parkhurst **Sir Francis Boynton 8th Bt.** m. Sally Bucktrout **Sir Henry Boynton 9th Bt.** m. Mary Gray
(1769-1801) (1777-1832) (1778-1854)

Louisa Strickland m. (1) **Sir Henry Boynton 10th Bt.** m. (2) Harriet Lightfoot Rev. Griffith Boynton m. Selina Watkins 2 sons & 6 daughters
(1811-1869)

Sir Henry (Somerville) Boynton 11th Bt. m. Mildred Paget Sir Griffith Boynton 12th Bt. m Euphemia Rev. Charles Boynton
(1844-1899) (1849-1937) Chalmers (1853-1928)
m. Mary Constance Cunliffe-Lister

Cycely Mabel m. Capt. Thomas Wickham Sir Griffith Boynton 13th Bt. m. Naomi Nightingale
(1877-1947) (assumed name Wickham-Boynton) (1884-1966)

Henry Wickham-Boynton **Marcus Wickham-Boynton** son, died in infancy
(1900-1942) (1904-1989)
(gave Hall to Preservation Trust)

Sir Philip Lloyd-Greame m. Mary Boynton
(1884-1972) (d.1974)
(assumed name Cunliffe-Lister:
later created Earl of Swinton)

John Cunliffe-Lister m. Ann Medlicott
(1916-1942)

David, 2nd Earl of Swinton m. Susan Sinclair Hon. Nicholas Cunliffe-Lister m. Susan Whitelaw
(1937-) (Baroness Masham) (1939-) (1944-)

Lorna Mark Simon
(1968-) (1970-) (1977-)

THE SONS OF JACOB ON THE GREAT HALL SCREEN

Representations of the twelve sons of Jacob who became the founding fathers of the twelve tribes of Israel are in four groups of three in the recessed panels of the frieze of the wooden part of the screen and are shown in order of seniority from the left, i.e. Reuben, Simeon, Levi, Judah, Issachar, Zebulun, Dan Naphtali, Gad, Asher, Joseph and Benjamin. By each one is a scene showing an incident from his life and a scroll bearing a more or less rhyming verse apparently based on Jacob's last words to his sons, Genesis Ch.49. In many cases the ends of lines do not coincide with ends of words, some letters, and in the case of Judah the whole last line apart from the first letter, are missing and letters have often been elided e.g. AND might be shown as A*D. The following is as it appears on the screen.

RUBEN   BEHOLD THE POT
              THE BEARE THE BED
              DO NOT STEM THE
              LUST OF
              RUBEN AND WCON
              STANT HEAD WHO
                WA   ACC
              OUNT

SIMION   THE HARE IN WOMANS MO
              UTH THE FACE THE
              SWORD THE WOL
              THE CAP AL THES
              PAINT OUT TH
              E ENVIOUS RAC THAT
              RUN TO THE MERM
                ISHA

LEVI   THIS IN BE UTY
              TRAC NOT
              C   CH YE PREACHERS OF GODS WORD
              FOR WHAT THIN
              K ELS HE WETH
              SUN AND MOONE DAM
              E VENUS WOLFE AND SWORD

JUDUS   LO HEARE
              THE BLESSED PRINCELY
              I SW OF JUDAS I
              OFFERING NOT H
              MATE THE OE P
              THE LION AND CROSS
              N

SACHAR   LEARN HEARE A
          SIMPLE LIFE NOT
          VOID OF PAYNE
          BUT STRIFE THE
          SITHE THE SPADE
          THE ASS SET FOR
          TH   WHAT MA
          N HE WAS

ZABULON THE POORE MAN
         AT HOME ZABULON
         FED THE STRANGER
         UNKNOWN ALS
         O CLOTHED WHE
         SHIP DID SAILE
         GOD DID NOT FAILE
         BUT GAVE HIM
         WIT TO GOVERN

DAN   THE SERPENT WITH
         WEAPON AND DAN DECLARE
         THE INTENT OF THESE MEN
         THAT WRATHFUL ARE

NEPTALI RUN NEPTALI M
         RACE BUT RUN
         APACE EMBRACE
         HIS GOODNESS
         TRUST IN   SU
         YOUR STATE YOU
         SE   SERVANTES
         TO BE THEN

GAD   YOU THAT E
         XCEL IN MAR
         TIAL FEATES
         NOT GAD BUT GO
         D OBEY LEAST
         IN GADS WRATH YOU GOD OFFE
         ND AND LOSE YOU
         R HOPE D PRA

ASER   TWO WAYS
         SAITH ASER
         ARE PREPARED
         FOR MEN THE
         ONE FOR JOY TH
         E LAST FOR DE
         ATH THE FIRST
         IS BLEST BUT

THIS BRA
DS S OR PAINE

JOSEPH   *LET JOSEPH TE*
EACH THE LOVE
AND CHASTITY
SO SHALT THOU
HAVE A BLESS
ED LONG LIFE
VOYD OF STRI
FE UNTO   THEM

BENJAMIN *DO MEAN AS YOUTH*
AND LOVERS BE
IS IN HEART AND
NOT IN LUST AS HERE
YOU PLAYNELY SE

THE GREAT HALL SCREEN

Of all the representational carving in the house the most concentrated is on the Great Hall Screen with its extraordinarily overcrowded mix of contemporary (c.1600), biblical, classical and allegorical figures.

Such figures are identified by their symbols or 'attributes', accompanying objects or animals, which have come to be recognised as belonging to them. As the same symbol is often associated with more than one 'owner' and, as we know, the Burton Agnes carvers sometimes got it wrong, sorting out the iconography can be a tricky business.

The frieze to the wooden part is relatively easy to decipher as most of the figures are named. On the plasterwork, of the free-standing figures on the top, the middle one may be Truth and Charity is certainly second from right but the rest are so far a mystery.

The architecture on the framed tier below would appear to represent the New Jerusalem, with angels, as described in the Book of Revelations, and men and women (most characteristically the pilgrim, centre,) approaching it.

On the narrow tier the pilgrim is again centre and all the rest, except the figure on the far right, can be identified as one of the 12 apostles.

The broad tier below has the four evangelists in the main panels. Also, from the left, are female figures who may represent four of the Seven Liberal Arts; the patriarchal figure with staff, far right, could be Moses which leaves the two males in contemporary dress for whom no convincing explanation has yet been offered.

The diagram below is of the wooden frieze and bottom two tiers of plasterwork with known figures in bold and surmised in italics.

	GEOMETRY	*GRAMMAR*	JAMES THE LESS
	BLANK		PAUL
	SIBYLLA AGRIPPA / SIBYLLA UBICA	*LOGIC*	JUDE
	DIFIDENTIA	ST. MATTHEW	SIMON
	REUBEN SIMEON LEVI		
HONOR	PAX	*ASTRONOMY*	ANDREW
	JUDAH ISSACHAR ZEBULON	ST. MARK	JOHN
	SIBYLLA PERSIA / SIBYLLA HELIOPA	*RHETORIC*	PILGRIM KNIGHT
	FOEDUS	ST. LUKE	PETER
	DAN NAPTHALI GAD		
LIBERAL-ITAS	CONCORDIA		JAMES THE GREATER
	ASHER JOSEPH BENJAMIN	ST. JOHN	BARTHOLOMEW
	OBEDIENTIA		
	SIBYLLA FRIGIA / SIBYLLA SAMIA		THOMAS
	PIETAS	*MOSES*	
	POTEST- ? AS		PHILIP
	INIQUITUDO		

THE OLD MANOR HOUSE

Some time before the wash house facilities were transferred to it round about 1712 most of the extra rooms which had been added to the Norman Manor house had been demolished and the breaches in its thick old walls filled in. Now it was considerably pulled about again. A new doorway was made at the north end of the east wall facing the back door of the main house and from it a straight flight of stairs led to the first floor. An extra storey was inserted above the first-floor great hall giving a sort of attic, perhaps sleeping accommodation for the laundry women.

In time either the washing was sent out or it was done back in the big house and the house and its remaining outbuildings, alias a rather grand Queen Anne laundry, began an ignominious new life as a general purpose store — cum — coal-house and began to decay through lack of care as nobody valued it.

Eventually it became unsafe and was in danger of being pulled down. Fortunately at this point Marcus Wickham-Boynton came on the scene and gave it to the National Trust who passed it on to the then Ministry of Works; in 1948 a lengthy programme of restoration was started for the most part using local labour from the village.

The structure was made sound by pouring tons of cement into the walls. Many of the 15th century king-post roof beams, which were riddled with death-watch beetle, were carefully replaced with matching woodwork and the lead was likewise renewed.

The vaulting in the north-west corner of the undercroft had been largely destroyed by the installation of the laundry stairs and this was rebuilt. In several other places the chalk ribs were badly decayed and were replaced with a form of plastic stone. The spiral staircase was rediscovered and made usable.

Outside the 17th century roof to the well housing was repaired as was the donkey wheel but from the time the local pumping station was built, upon the arrival of the mains water supply in 1938, the well has been dry.

As there had been no possibility of replacing the 18th century brick skin and windows, though the woodwork in the latter was renewed, the building remains a hybrid with a very misleading outward appearance not preparing one for the Norman structure within.

Unlike the Hall the Norman Manor House is open throughout the year, with the exception of some public holidays, and the Keyholder is Mr. Keith Hawkins, the Burton Agnes estate maintenance superviser, who did much of the woodwork restoration as a young man. The building is now in the care of the Department of the Environment which, at the time of writing (1993), is anxious to shed many of its responsibilities and ownership may revert to the estate.

THE ESTATE

The money brought by the 19th century Boynton spouses kept the family in comfort but it did not fundamentally affect the economics of the estate which continued to get smaller as the manors of Roxby, Barmston. Haisthorpe and other properties were successively sold off. Now, however, the position is sound and the Burton Agnes estate stretches to about 4,000 acres of which 2,000 is in hand and the rest tenanted.

The village is still recognisably an estate village although some houses have been sold off and there are some council houses. The earliest dated house was built by the sixth baronet in 1767 but there are some older ones remaining. The tenth baronet rebuilt quite a number in 1857 and others were built by the Wickham-Boyntons between 1912 and 1938. Elizabeth Boynton's almshouses survived until 1939 when they, and most of the oldest houses then standing in the village, were pulled down when the crossroads were widened. The later houses are strung out along the Bridlington Road.

Other roads have been altered from time to time to suit the needs of the owner. The Rudston road achieved its present position in 1861.

Away from the busy main road the village is a quiet place now with just a joiner, a blacksmith, and one general store-cum-post office. In 1881 there were also two tailors, two dressmakers, brickmakers and a 'rabbit butcher' amongst others together with the school master, station master and porter. Though trains continue to run between Hull and Scarborough the Burton Agnes station is closed. The school still thrives, however, and the children dance round the maypole on the front lawn of the Hall at the annual Garden Gala carrying on a village tradition; the Hall car park is on land once known as Maypole Hill.

The village pond fed, it was thought, from inexhaustible springs and the reason for the original settlement of Burton Agnes, has become a problem; unusually dry winters and excessive water extraction have caused a drop in the water table and the virtual drying up of the pond each summer to everyone's consternation including the local press. The poor ducks and other waterfowl which inhabit it stand disconsolately in ankle deep muddy water for part of the year. Expensive attempts to pump up water from deeper strata have been only partially successful. The mere was drained and turned into agricultural land around about 1900.

But the house, now very much part of the country's leisure industry, flourishes and is the favourite historic building of many people including those with a professional interest. What is so special about Burton Agnes Hall? There are older houses, grander houses, houses that have original furniture and original kitchens on display, that have been the scene of events of national importance but still people prefer Burton Agnes and come back time after time. They say it is a friendly house, even a homely house because it is indeed a home, and it is so well cared for. It is full of beautiful things and you can take your time looking at them because, best of all, it is never crowded. And, who knows, if you are lucky you might just see the ghost!

FAMILY TREE OF THE FOUNDERS OF THE AMERICAN BOYNTONS

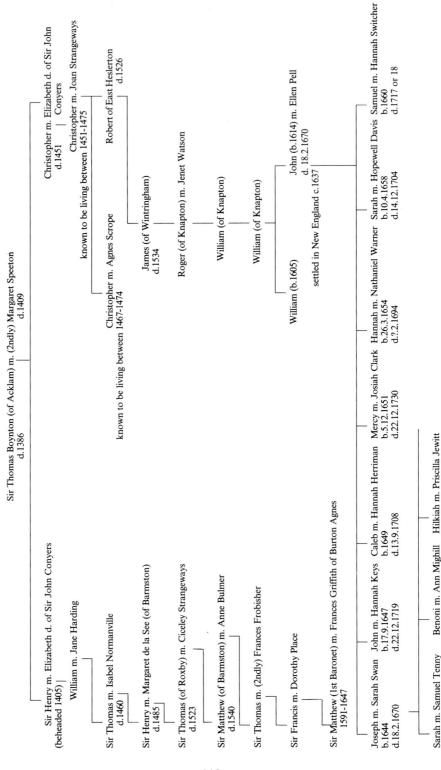

Sir Thomas Boynton (of Acklam) m. (2ndly) Margaret Speeton
d.1386

Christopher m. Elizabeth d. of Sir John
d.1451 | Conyers

Christopher m. Joan Strangeways

known to be living between 1451-1475

Robert of East Heslerton
d.1526

Sir Henry m. Elizabeth d. of Sir John Conyers
(beheaded 1405) |

William m. Jane Harding

Christopher m. Agnes Scrope

known to be living between 1467-1474

James (of Wintringham)
d.1534

Roger (of Knapton) m. Jenet Watson

William (of Knapton)

William (of Knapton)

Sir Thomas m. Isabel Normanville
d.1460

Sir Henry m. Margaret de la See (of Barmston)
d.1485

Sir Thomas (of Roxby) m. Ciceley Strangeways
d.1523

Sir Matthew (of Barmston) m. Anne Bulmer
d.1540

Sir Thomas m. (2ndly) Frances Frobisher

William (b.1605)

John (b.1614) m. Ellen Pell
d. 18.2.1670

settled in New England c.1637

Sir Francis m. Dorothy Place

Sir Matthew (1st Baronet) m. Frances Griffith of Burton Agnes
1591-1647

Mercy m. Josiah Clark
b.5.12.1651
d.22.12.1730

Caleb m. Hannah Herriman
b.1649
d.13.9.1708

Hannah m. 26.3.1654
b.26.3.1654
d.?.2.1694

Nathaniel Warner

Sarah m. Hopewell Davis
b.10.4.1658
d.14.12.1704

Samuel m. Hannah Switcher
b.1660
d.1717 or 18

Joseph m. Sarah Swan
b.1644
d.18.2.1670

John m. Hannah Keys
b.17.9.1647
d.22.12.1719

Hilkiah m. Priscilla Jewitt

Sarah m. Samuel Tenny

Benoni m. Ann Mighill

118

THE AMERICAN CONNECTION

Had Sir Frances Boynton succceeded in emigrating to New England in the 1630s the history of Burton Agnes Hall might have been very different. However his distant cousins, the brothers William (b.1605) and John (b.1614) Boynton, did go out either under his auspices or independently and from them descend the American Boyntons. They were members of a younger branch of the family who probably have as their founding ancestor Christopher, the second son of Sir Thomas Boynton of Acklam (d.1386), — Matthew's line comes through the eldest — and which seems to have lived successively in Sedbury near Richmond, Wintringham and Knapton, all in North Yorkshire.

However John Boynton has a strong connection with East Yorkshire for after he married Ellen Pell of Boston he went to live in Rowley, Massachusetts, the settlement founded by the Rev. Ezekiel Rogers, the dissenting minister of Rowley, a village about 8 miles north east of Hull. Rogers led a group of twenty families which sailed to America from that town in 1639. Joseph, the first of John and Ellen Boynton's children, was born in 1644 and at least three of his children married into families of the Rogers group — Sarah Boynton to Samuel Tenny, Benoni Boynton to Ann Mighill and Hilkiah Boynton to Priscilla Jewett. There are numerous Boyntons now living in the United States many of whom like to visit Burton Agnes when in this country.

PRINCIPAL SOURCES

Allison, K. J., *Burton Agnes. Victoria County History. York, East Riding, Vol. II,* Oxford University Press, London. 1974

Binn, J., *Scarborough and the Civil Wars.* Northern History. Vol. XXII 1986

Collier, C. V., *An Account of the Boynton Family.* Published by the author. Middlesbrough. 1914

English, B. *The Great Landowners of East Yorkshire 1530 – 1910.* Harvester Wheatsheaf. 1990

English, B., *The Lords of Holderness.* Oxford University Press. 1979

Fiennes, C., *Through Yorkshire on a side-saddle in the time of William and Mary.* Fuld and Tuer, Leadenhall Press, London. Reprinted in Old Yorkshire, ed. William Smith. Longmans Green & Co. London. 1891

Forster, G. C. F., *The East Riding Justices of the Peace in the 17th C.* East Yorkshire Local History Society. 1973

Girouard, M., *Life in the English Country House.* Penguin. 1980

Cliffe, J. T., *The Yorkshire Gentry.* University of London Historical Studies. Athlone Press. 1969

Hill, C., *The Century of Revolution, 1603 – 1714.* Van Nostrand Reinhold (UK) Co. Ltd. 1980

Pevsner, N., *The Buildings of England. Yorkshire: York and the East Riding.* Penguin Books. 1978

Roebuck, P., *Yorkshire Baronets 1640 – 1760.* University of Hull. 1980

Witty, J. R., *A History of Beverley Grammar School.* [Beverley Grammar School].

Wood, M., *Burton Agnes Old Manor House.* Ministry of Works. 1956

Wood, M., *The English Mediaeval House.* Bracken Books. London. 1990

Tatenhill Parish Register Vol. 1 Births Deaths & Marriages 1563 — 1689. Staffordshire Record Office.

Alrewas Parish Register. Staffordshire Record Office.

Burton Agnes Parish Register. Humberside County Archive Office.

Documents (DDWB) deposited in Hull University Archives by Crust Todd Mills & Co. at the request of Mr. Marcus Wickham-Boynton.